MATTHEW PARKER
AND
HIS BOOKS

MATTHEW PARKER AND HIS BOOKS

Sandars Lectures in Bibliography
Delivered on 14, 16, and 18 May 1990
at the
University of Cambridge

by

R. I. Page

photographs by

Mildred Budny

Medieval Institute Publications
in association with
The Research Group on Manuscript Evidence,
The Parker Library
Corpus Christi College, Cambridge

WESTERN MICHIGAN UNIVERSITY

Kalamazoo, Michigan
1993

Library of Congress Cataloging-in-Publication Data

Page, R. I. (Raymond Ian)
Matthew Parker and his books : Sandars lectures in bibliography delivered on 14, 16, and 18 May 1990 at the University of Cambridge / by R.I. Page ; photographs by Mildred Budny.
p. cm.
Includes bibliographical references.
ISBN 978-1-879288-20-1
1. Parker, Matthew, 1504-1575--Library. 2. Book collecting--England--History--16th century. 3. Manuscripts--Collectors and collecting--England--History--16th century. 4. English language--Old English, ca. 450-1100--Research--England--History. 5. Corpus Christi College (University of Cambridge). Library--History--16th century. I. Title. II. Title: Sandars lectures in bibliography.
Z997.P246P34 1993
002'.074--dc20 93-1097
CIP

Printed and bound by CPI Group (UK) Ltd, Croydon, CR0 4YY

Cover design by Linda K. Judy

To the Memory of Three Fine Scholars

whose work illuminated the Parker Library

Patrick Bury
Christopher Cheney
Bruce Dickins

Contents

ILLUSTRATIONS

(Unless otherwise noted, all illustrations appear at actual size)

Following Page 107

49a, b	Parker used the MS CCCC 452 text of Eadmer's *Historia novorum* (a) in the compilation of his work (b)
50a, b	Parker's cross-reference in printed text of *A defence of priestes mariages* (a) refers to marginal notation in MS CCCC 452 (b)
51a, b	Parker's cryptic marginal reference to "Pecham" on p. 328 of *A defence of priestes mariages* (a) and corresponding marginal comment in MS CCCC 342 (b)
52	John Joscelyn's annotations in MS CCCC 191
53	Sixteenth-century annotation of verses by Prosper of Aquitaine in printed book B.4.16
54	One of Parker's proof corrections to his translation of Prosper's verses, MS CCCC 448
55	MS CCCC 198, the *A testimonie of antiquitie* homily, marked up in margin to correspond to printed text
56	The Easter homily (MS CCCC 162) cross-referenced in the margin to the printed text of *A testimonie . . .*
57	A supply leaf for MS CCCC 178, probably in Matthew Parker's hand
58a, b	An extract from MS CCCC 144, the *Corpus Glossary* (a) and an extract from MS CCCC 183, a glossary of difficult Latin words with Latin or Old English equivalents (b)
59	An extract from MS CCCC 449, Ælfric's *Glossary*
60	An extract from MS CCCC 178, the Rule of St. Benedict in Latin and Old English
61	An extract from MS CCCC 198, where the "tremulous Worcester hand" errs in translating Old English
62	An extract from the text and translation of Alfred's preface to his version of the *Cura pastoralis*, as appended to some issues of Asser's *Life of Alfred*
63	An extract from MS CCCC 197A, an anonymous translation of Alfred's preface to the *Cura pastoralis*

FOREWORD

This book comprises the three lectures that I delivered as Sandars Reader in Bibliography before the University of Cambridge on 14, 16, 18 May 1990. I have made few changes in the text as read, only tidying away some repetitions and removing colloquialisms more suited to the spoken than to the written word. I have deliberately avoided the practice—one common among those who print lecture texts—of supplying extensive bibliographical annotation to each page, a practice illustrative less of the lecturer's erudition than of his easy access to a computerized bibliography; moreover a practice devised to avoid the pain of using judgment to determine what to put in, what to leave out. Despite my principles I have added a few of the more important references for those who want to follow them up.

My text betrays its oral origins in being not completely consistent in style throughout, usually for reasons of convenience, sometimes no doubt through inadvertence. In quoting sixteenth-century Latin I have expanded abbreviations silently in most cases. This could not be detected in a spoken version, but it adds an element of interpretation to the evidence in a printed one. Sixteenth-century scribes are often erratic and self-contradictory in their usages, and it is hard to present their material precisely save by using more pedantic methods than are appropriate in such a work as this. Silent expansion is the practical solution, but readers should be warned of it. The question of whether to translate Latin (in addition to quoting it) or not has exercised me, and again I have, inconsistently, translated only the more significant passages, leaving others in the decent obscurity of a learned language.

It will be evident to readers that I am not a trained bibliographer; only an engineer turned student of Old English. Thus my lectures are the reaction of an amateur bibliographer and librarian faced with a collection of books of immense importance, value, rarity, and variety. Inevitably my lectures contain a good deal of personal opinion, some might even suspect prejudice, which I hope the reader will take in good part. In particular my comments on those professionals, sometimes called scholars, who arrogantly ignore the difficulties that face the librarian who has to balance openness against security; those who loudly demand rights while averting their eyes from responsibilities.

I am very happy to express my thanks to the Syndics of the University Library, Cambridge, for electing me to the Sandars Readership and so giving me the opportunity of reporting on some of the work we have done in the Parker Library over a couple of decades. Also the University Librarian and his staff, and the librarians and staffs of Gonville & Caius and Trinity Colleges and of Trinity Hall for their help in assembling materials. In particular I must acknowledge with gratitude the encouragement, forbearance, and loyalty of the staff of the Parker Library. I recognize too the patience shown by the Master and Fellows of Corpus Christi College during my long tenure of the Parker Librarianship. Their ordeal is now at an end.

It will be evident that much of what I say in these lectures represents work in progress. Already I have gone beyond them here and there, as part of the work of the Research Group on Manuscript Evidence of the Parker Library. The Trustees of the Leverhulme Fund have been most generous in their support of this research, and I take this opportunity of expressing my gratitude. My debt to my colleagues and associates of the Research Group is acknowledged in the final lecture of the series. I reiterate it here.

R. I. Page
Corpus Christi College,
Cambridge

ACKNOWLEDGEMENT

The author and publisher express their gratitude to the Master and Fellows of Corpus Christi College, Cambridge, and to Dr. M. O. Budny for permission to publish the photographs that accompany the lectures.

A MIGHTY COLLECTOR OF BOOKS

The protagonist of these lectures is Matthew Parker, successively Bible Clerk, Fellow, and Master of Corpus Christi College, Cambridge; Archbishop of Canterbury to Queen Elizabeth I, proponent of the settlement of the Church of England, and enthusiast for that "holy mediocrity" which still, in one sense or another, characterizes its episcopacy; prelate, theologian, administrator, translator, publisher, but principally in this present context, bibliophile. He was not, I think, an easy or a happy man. John Strype, the eighteenth-century historian and biographer, sums him up: "He was a Man of Stomach, and in a good Cause feared no body. . . . And because he wanted a complying, flattering, complaisant Temper and Carriage, he procured to himself many powerful Enemies." One knows the feeling.

> His Learning, though it were universal, yet it ran chiefly upon Antiquity, In so much that he was one of the greatest Antiquarians of the Age. And the World is for ever beholden to him for two things; *Viz.*, for retrieving many antient Authors, *Saxon* and *British*, as well as *Norman*, and for restoring and enlightening a great deal of the antient History of this noble Island.

And again: "Indeed he was the chief Retriever of that our ancient Native Language, the *Saxon* I mean, and encouraged heartily the Study of it." And finally: "He was therefore a mighty Collector of Books, to preserve, as much as could be, the antient Monuments of the learned Men of our Nation from perishing" (Strype 1711:524, 528, 535).

It is as a collector of books that I want to view him first, for much of his collection survives in the library I have had the honor to keep for a quarter of a century. The tale of how Parker's books came to Corpus Christi has been often told, and I allude to it here only as an opening to my theme. Parker had collected printed books and manuscripts for much of his life and manuscripts particularly since the Privy Council's broadsheet of 1568 authorizing him to take possession of "auncient recordes or monumentes written" so that they could be examined and recorded. He made several attempts to provide for the disposition of his library after his death, the latest being a quadripartite indenture, dated 1 January 1574 (17 Elizabeth=1575), made between the archbishop and the masters and fellows of three Cambridge colleges, Corpus Christi, Gonville and Caius, and Trinity Hall. The books were to be held by Corpus, but subject to audit every year by the master and one scholar of each of the other colleges: they had the power to require any stray books to be replaced, to fine Corpus for missing items, and if there were serious losses *per . . . supinam negligentiam*, (through idle neglect) to assign the whole collection (on the agreement of the Vice-Chancellor and a senior doctor of the University) to Caius, who would take over the same duties. If Caius failed in its task, the library would pass to Trinity Hall, and so round the group again.

For such an arrangement to be viable, audit lists were needed, and Parker supplied three, one for each college, to be used turn and turn about. (To my knowledge there are three further primary lists, and may be more: I know of those in British Library, Royal App.66, in Lambeth Palace Library, MS 723, and in Cambridge University Library, MS Add.2589. These I leave aside for the present purpose. There are presumably a number of secondary lists, as in British Library, Burney 362, made for the circle of Isaac Casaubon.) With official lists like those still held by the three colleges, it should be easy enough to define Matthew Parker's library precisely. But things are seldom so simple in Cambridge, *a fortiori* in Corpus Christi.

Here it is necessary to describe the audit lists briefly. I take my account from CCCC MS 575, the Corpus Christi copy of Matthew Parker's Register of Books. This divides into two main sections. The first is an inventory of books in the larger library, *in maiore bibliotheca*, also called "the outward library." These are all large format printed books, divided into sections according to subject matter. For each book there is a general title, the number of volumes, the size (here usually folio), the type of binding (in wood—*lig*—or card—*car*) and the date of binding. (Plate 1) The second section comprises books in the smaller library, *in minore bibliotheca*, also called "the inward library." These are more confusedly arranged under a series of letters or numbers, or "Standinge on the shelues within the Lockers as heare directed by seauen figures," or "Bookes in parchment closures as the lye on heapes," or a group of *Miscellanea* marked "Theis to be kept within the little Librarie." The books in the little library comprehend both manuscripts and printed books. For manuscripts the Register gives a title and an *incipit*, the opening words not necessarily of the first text but of what the compiler considered the first significant text. The printed books are defined by format (usually quarto or octavo but sometimes smaller), binding (wood, card, or parchment—*perg*), and printing date. Thus the Register provides the material for identifying each book in Parker's library, at any rate in theory. But theory is not practice.

There are a number of difficulties in these registers. (1) The three official lists do not always agree, and it is hard to see how an authoritative audit could be carried out with lists that had discrepancies. I think the Corpus copy shows the most wear of the three, and perhaps this was commonly taken as the official register despite the provisions of the indenture. (2) The lists show common alterations, with items erased, altered, or added. Thus they represent a particular state of Parker's library, perhaps that of c.1574. Some of the items erased can be supplied from the Royal manuscript of the Register, which therefore records an earlier state of the collection. (3) Added to each college copy of the Register is a note signed by John Parker, Matthew's eldest son, admitting that when he came to check his father's library some of the books were missing, "either lent or embeceled"—one knows the feeling—so the college was not responsible for their loss. (Plate 2) Hence a number of items in the Register are annotated as missing and initialed

"JP," often with some added phrase like "wanting at the first bringing," or simply and laconically *deest* (not there). (Plate 3) John's annotations are not always correct. Occasionally an item is marked missing though it can still be traced on the library shelves. Some items were entered twice in different parts of the Register, and John deleted one entry. (4) Apparently the Register lists were soon found to be inaccurate. The Corpus copy has, stuck to an opening flyleaf, a paper list in a sixteenth-century hand marked "Bookes not agreing with the originall copye." (Plate 4) It corrects a dozen of the items in the audit lists in terms such as: "Hierome is in borde, not paste, and it was printed Anno 1516. not 1532." Or "Austine is but in 8.vol. onlye, not in 9.vol: & yeare 1541. not 1543." Or more generally: "Brentius in Lucam, do not agree." Or "The two Decretales cum apparatu, be not right figured." And so on. There are only twelve corrections in this list; there should have been many more.

Before I come to the contents, a couple of further notes on the catalogue's structure. Within the first group of books, those in the greater library, there are two types of subdivision. Lines are left blank at irregular intervals, presumably indicating some distinction that I have not yet traced. Added to the original lists but clearly at an early date is a division into twelve numbered sections which seem to represent presses or lockers in which the books were kept. To this extent the registers were practical ones, available to check off the volumes in order on their shelves.

Now to the contents. I begin with manuscripts, and it is useful to start with those in the group labelled *Miscellanea.* These are composite codices, each with a variety of material brought together from diverse sources. The advantage of taking them first is that the Register defines them in greater detail than the other manuscripts. It lists their contents more completely, adds the pagination of items, and almost every entry ends by giving the total number of pages in the manuscript. For example, that for *Miscellanea C* (=CCCC 102) catalogues the eleven pieces of theological discussion or controversy, and ends "Hic liber continet pag:543:" which happens to be correct. In contrast, *Miscellanea A* (=CCCC 113) is said to have 429 pages. There is indeed a break of content at pp. 429/30 but the manuscript now continues to 446 pages, with the distinctive Parkerian red crayon page numbering uninterrupted.

The last two items of this manuscript were added after the register entry was drawn up and are also not included in the Parkerian contents list attached to the opening of the book. They are a late addition indeed. *Miscellanea B* (=CCCC 105) is said to have 425 pages, but it has 458 (the last two folios unnumbered), including three added items. The red numbering reaches to 453, and the manuscript's Parkerian contents list was clearly compiled in several stages. The Register lists *Miscellanea Q* (=CCCC 100) as having 401 pages, the number written over an erasure. The contents slip at the front of the book is uncertain, giving three figures, 568, 401, 342, the first two crossed out; in fact 342 is the correct number. Its list has an entry for p. 365 crossed through and unreadable. There is the further complexity in this manuscript that its pages 261–323 have a second, and apparently earlier, red crayon numbering 1–6[3].

In all these cases pages have been supplied to or removed from the ends of composite codices, or pages have been shifted round within them. Even more confusing is the case of *Miscellanea G* (=CCCC 111). Elsewhere I have argued that pages, including some printed material, were inserted into the middle of that manuscript, though again the page numbering continues more or less uninterrupted. Clearly the miscellaneous manuscripts deserve thorough study, with batches of paper distinguished by their water marks to try to detect how they were put together. Often with these manuscripts the Parker Register records an earlier state than the present one, even though the present state *is* Parkerian as the continuity of pagination shows. Two important conclusions derive from these observations: (1) The annual audit must have been less rigorous than Parker had planned. His regulations provide for the college being fined for the loss of individual pages of a manuscript, but this could hardly apply when the Register clearly listed the wrong number of pages. If the college were fined for losing pages, could it be rewarded for having more pages than the Register defined? That would only be fair. (2) Composite manuscripts were in a state of confusion in Parker's lifetime. We must assume they were disbound, perhaps more than once. It is not safe, therefore, to draw conclusions from their present states. But this uncertainty might apply to other manuscripts also. Indeed, any Register entry for any manuscript should be scrutinized before being accepted.

This conclusion affects some of the major manuscripts of Parker's collection. I give two striking examples:

(A) One of the most important of Corpus's earlier manuscripts is that commonly referred to as the *Parker Chronicle and Laws* (=CCCC 173). In fact this is now a composite manuscript. Its first part is indeed the famous early text of the *Anglo-Saxon Chronicle* (a primary source for the early history of England) together with the laws of Alfred and Ine and some related material. This was compiled over many years, between the end of the ninth and the eleventh centuries. However, bound to it is a completely different book—different in format, content, and size. This is an eighth-century manuscript whose first and main item is the *Carmen Paschale* of the fifth-century poet Caelius Sedulius. This was once a quite elegant codex which was put to use at various times throughout the Anglo-Saxon period and eventually declined to the status of a school book, subject to all the indignities that a school book suffers. The two parts of CCCC 173 have little in common, though paleographers claim to have identified one of the *Chronicle* scribes with a corrector who added to the Sedulius, whether rightly or not I do not know (Bishop 1966:248; Parkes 1976:156).

The Parker Register entry for this manuscript, under S. 11, is: (Plate 5)

Annales Saxonici ecclesie Cantuariensis	}	willelm cyng
Leges Aluredi regis.		

There is thus no mention of the Sedulius. Of course, this could be because the account of the manuscript's contents was deliberately left incomplete, being adequate as it stood to identify the volume on the shelf; or, taking a line through the *Miscellanea*, it could be because the Register records a state of the *Chronicle* manuscript before it was bound with the Sedulius. I am now inclined to think the second. If this is the case, the link between the *Chronicle* manuscript and the Sedulius could be chance, the effect of the caprice of the sixteenth-century collector or binder. The identification of the common scribal hand in the two parts of CCCC 173 is thus crucial and needs scrutiny. It has been questioned (Dumville 1987:164).

The red crayon page numbering does not help in this manuscript because it does not continue throughout: indeed, it does not reach even to the end of the *Chronicle* section. All we know further is that in 1600, when T(homas) J(ames) printed his catalogue of the Corpus manuscripts in *Ecloga Oxonio-Cantabrigiensis,* the Sedulius was bound with the *Chronicle and Laws* and, if James was precise here, *between* the *Chronicle* and the *Laws* (James 1600: I, 89). When Wanley recorded the manuscript in 1705 the Sedulius was in its present position, bound after the *Chronicle and Laws* (Wanley 1705:130). I would guess that the uniting of these two disparate manuscripts was a late Parkerian idea and that at the same time Parker cut away the original page 1 of the *Chronicle* text (with its incipit *willelm cyng*) so as to give a tidier opening to his book. Then (?) he wrote at the top of page 3 the present title, "chronica scripta anno 23 etatis alfredi / Annales Saxonici." (Plate 6)

Why then were the two manuscripts united? I cannot be sure, but I can put forward a theory. In 1574, in the last year of his life, Matthew Parker was preparing a text of Asser's life of Alfred the Great for publication. We cannot tell how much of the work he did himself since the manuscript of this history (British Library, Cotton Otho A.xii) went up in the fire of 1731, so its text is now known only from sixteenth-century transcripts and printed editions. However, close to the opening of the *Life* Asser quotes a passage from Sedulius's *Carmen Paschale,* indeed a set of lines that occurs on the first page of the Sedulius text of MS 173. Since, as we have seen, Parker connected the *Anglo-Saxon Chronicle* of CCCC 173 with the name of Alfred, he may have thought the Sedulius an appropriate manuscript to unite with it. We have a Parkerian transcript of the Otho A.xii text of Asser (CCCC 100, fols. 325–62), and the Sedulius quotation shows Parker's red crayon underlining.

(B) My second example involves the splendid eighth-century Gospel Book fragment, parts of John and Luke, which for convenience can be called the Corpus Gospels (now CCCC 197B). Until recently this Gospel Book was the second part of a composite codex, CCCC 197, whose first part was a collection of fourteenth- and fifteenth-century vellum and paper manuscripts on historical topics. The entry for this manuscript in the Parker Register, M.14, reads:

De Johanna le pusil
Chronica Jo: Malvernensis
Articuli Ri: Scroope } Vniversis presentes

This roughly sums up the first part of the manuscript (now CCCC 197A) though the items are not in their present order, but there is no mention of the Gospels. CCCC 197A now opens with the Parkerian contents list, and that puts the items of part one in their present order, and adds: "ffragmenta quedam novi testamenti in veteri scripto." Each item is given a red crayon page reference, the Gospels beginning on p. 245 which agrees with the running red page numbering within the book itself.

It would appear then that M.14 as recorded in the Register was disbound, its items rearranged, the Gospel fragments added, and the whole rebound and paginated, all within Parker's time. Before this, however, the Gospel Book may have been adapted to form a volume of its own. At any rate, its opening had been tampered with to present an impressive title page. It now begins with a frontispiece picturing the eagle of St. John, followed by a display page of the first words of the Gospel, *In principio eret* (sic) *uerbum*. Originally these two pages faced one another. At some stage before the red crayon page numbering was added, the eagle page was reversed to turn its back on the opening words of the Gospel rather than face them. In Parker's terms this would serve for the beginning of a volume, as would Parker's note at the top of the eagle page, "fragmentum quatuor euangeliorum. Hic Liber olim missus a Gregorio papa ad augustinum archiepiscopum: sed nuper sic mutilatus." (Plate 7) It is even possible that the ordering of the Gospels, John before Luke, is a Parkerian rearrangement. For Luke there survives no symbol or display page; it could not provide so magnificent a frontispiece.

In this opening section I have tried to show what a blunt instrument the Parker Register is for determining the extent and nature of Parker's manuscript collection. The manuscripts—whatever their origin—are in a sense sixteenth-century ones; at any rate they are likely to be affected, sometimes severely, by sixteenth-century collecting practices. There is the further complication that Parker's contemporary bindings do not survive in the manuscripts he gave into Corpus's keeping. A few medieval bindings are still to be found in our manuscript collection, but the later bindings were largely replaced in the mid-eighteenth century in a hasty and comprehensive piece of conservation. Then, as the cataloguer James Nasmith complained, *operculis bibliopegi incuria abjectis multa hujusmodi indicia perierunt* (through the binder's carelessness covers were thrown away and many similar bits of evidence perished [Nasmith 1777:277]). Presumably things like opening pastedowns and contents lists were discarded, and with them much material we would now like to have.

And of course there is the further complication that not all Matthew Parker's manuscripts came to Corpus Christi. In 1574 he was persuaded to give twenty-five volumes (as well as many printed books) to the depleted University Library, and they remain there to the present day providing an interesting comparison with those that came to the college (Oates 1986:101–09). Others stayed in the possession of John Parker, for reasons I do not understand. Some others later found their way to Trinity College, Cambridge, for reasons I find even more difficult to understand. M. R. James traced eighteen of Parker's manuscript volumes there (James 1912:xxv). Others again went to the Royal Library and thence to the British Library, and yet others to private collections. The piquant thing is that Parker seems not always clear about what he wanted to go where. To take two examples:

(A) The second item under letter S is "Beda saxonice," the Old English translation of the Venerable Bede's *Ecclesiastical History*. The Register gives this the *incipit* "Gloriossissimo regi" which is hardly Old English: it is of course the opening of Bede's Latin dedicatory letter to King Ceolwulf of Northumbria. The only Old English Bede that Corpus holds is CCCC 41, and in consequence this has traditionally been identified with S.2. The catch is that this manuscript does not open with the Latin dedication, nor is there any evidence to suggest that one has been cut away at the beginning. There is some confusion here, and I think I know what it was. Parker had a second copy of the Old English Bede. In 1574 he gave it to the University Library: item 3 of his *Libri scripti*, now CUL MS Kk.3.18. After its list of chapters this has the opening dedicatory letter in Latin, beginning GLORIOSISSIMO REGI. It seems the two manuscripts were mixed up, though I do not know when or how. MS Kk.3.18 has all the appearance of a conventional Parkerian gift to the University Library, with on p. 1, the name "Matthæus Cantuar: 1574" at the top and "Continet pag. 193" at the foot. Thus there was not here a simple casual mistake on the part of some ignorant laborer—Parker saying, "Take my Old English Bede to the University Library," and the carrier picking up the wrong one. From the Register it looks as though Kk.3.18 (as it now is) should be part of the collection he intended for Corpus. But then what of CCCC 41? This manuscript presents a further difficulty. At the head of the opening page of its text, written in a pair of sixteenth- / seventeenth-century hands, is "Historia Bede / Collegij Corporis Christi Cantabrigie sum / incola." (Plate 8) Such an entry is, I think, unparalleled in Corpus manuscripts. If the evidence of printed books is anything to go by, the mention of the College at the beginning of a volume implies that it was the property of the society rather than of Parker. It would be hard to demonstrate this conclusively, but the implication is there.

(B) N.19 of the Register is "Gramatica Saxonica" with the *incipit* "Ego Elfricus," the grammar and glossary of the late tenth-century scholar Ælfric. A copy of this is now CCCC 449. However, Parker had two further copies of this work. One he gave to the University Library, no.23 of his *Libri scripti*, now CUL MS Hh.1.10. Another copy passed to John Parker, thence to Lumley, and is now British Library MS Royal 15 B xxii. All have the *incipit* "Ego Ælfricus," though in the CCCC 449 case it is on a sixteenth-century supply leaf. The difficulty with this group is that MS Royal 15 B xxii has on the first page proper of the text (fol. 5^r) the pencil inscription "Cor. Coll." which would normally indicate that this volume is the College's property. Again there was an opportunity for confusion here, and Parker's men seem to have seized it eagerly. In fact, however, there is a further confusion to be noted. John Parker had a second copy of Ælfric's grammar and glossary which was to become Trinity College, Cambridge, MS R.9.17. This has been identified with MS 40 of the list of John's books at Beakesbourne preserved in Lambeth Palace Library, MS 737 (Strongman 1977:16). It has the same *incipit* as the others, "Ego Ælfricus" on a supply leaf.

Before I leave the manuscripts, a final problem that my late great colleague Christopher Cheney drew renewed attention to in a recent article that shows all his splendid precision of thought and clarity of exposition: the question of the Markaunt manuscripts (Cheney 1987). In

1439 Thomas Markaunt, Fellow, left to Corpus Christi a gift of seventy-five volumes of books, listed in a catalogue that now forms part of CCCC 232. For full identification the books were catalogued with some precision, each given its second and penultimate folio *incipit*. From these details five manuscripts now in the Parker Library have been identified: Markaunt 15, *Gregorius super homilias*=CCCC 159; Markaunt 18, *Compendium veritatis theologice*=CCCC 64; Markaunt 21, *Liber diversorum tractatuum*=CCCC 275; Markaunt 31, *Brito*=CCCC 479; Markaunt 72, *Liber de apocalipsi in gallicis*=CCCC 394. (Plate 9) All these are included in Parker's Register and therefore now appear as part of the Parker bequest. From which we may note that the Register evidently contains books that can be shown to have been in the College's possession before Parker's time. Of course, we have all had the experience of finding on our shelves books that should be on someone else's; as well as the more melancholy experience of finding on someone else's shelves books that should be on ours. Why these Markaunt books were among Parker's I do not know. There are several possibilities, and I list two: (1) that he bought from the College outdated books they were disposing of; (2) that he included these volumes—perhaps all that then remained of Markaunt's bequest—so that they could be secured from being lost by the expedient of the annual audit. Whatever the reason, it is as well we are aware that Parker's list contains manuscripts that may, strictly speaking, not have been Parker's. And the same may apply to the printed books, though here it is harder to demonstrate.

And so to Parker's printed books, which of course outnumber the manuscripts. I am sometimes asked how many printed books Parker left to the College, and I usually give an evasive answer: "That depends on what you mean by a book." For the Register is not always helpful here. To take three examples.

(A) Under 18.6 (p. 80) the Register enters the title "Admonitio pauli tertij 16. 1548" (= SP 445). In fact this volume is a composite one. The named item is certainly in the volume, but it is not now the first entry and may never have been, for the book is still in its sixteenth-century binding—it is one of the "Bookes in parchment closures as the lye on heapes." It contains eight separate items published between 1534 and 1548, all on matters of religious or political dispute. Of one of them, *The enquirie and verdite of the quest panneld of the death of Richard Hune wich was founde hanged in Lolars Tower* published perhaps in Antwerp in 1537, this is the only complete copy to survive (STC 13970); of another, we have the only example of a particular variant; of two more items, one of only two recorded copies. Indeed, in modern terms the named book, *Admonitio paterna Pauli III . . . ad invictissimum Caesarem Carolum V* (Adams P 464), is perhaps the least interesting of all contents of the volume.

(B) The Register entry 5.7 (p. 71) reads simply "Zwinglius 8 1530" (=SP 415). This does not reveal that the volume has in fact eight separate pieces by several writers, Erasmus and Luther as well as Zwingli, all published on the Continent in the 1520s and 1530s.

(C) Occasionally the cataloguers got bored. So, the Register entry 19.10 (p. 80) says engagingly "Libelli varij vt in primo folio 8 1555" (=SP 447). Its first flyleaf has indeed a sixteenth-century list of the fourteen individual items that make up this volume. (Plate 10) It gives a running pagination of the title pages that corresponds to the Parkerian red crayon numbering in the volume. The collection is certainly various, with, for example, *An epitome of the title that the kynges maiestie of Englande, hath to the sovereigntie of Scotland* (STC 3196)—a burning topic—bound up with *The true report of the burnyng of the steple and churche of Poules in London* (STC 19930)—an even more burning topic—and the sole copy of this edition of *A proper newe booke of cokerye, declarynge what maner of meates be best in season, for al times in the yere,* irreverently known in Corpus Christi College as "Mrs. Parker's Cook Book" (STC 3366).

In effect these three Register titles I have examined comprise thirty separate publications. But there are other traps lying in wait for anyone who tries to define Parker's collection of printed books from the Register. Here again it is convenient to work from specific examples.

Printed book EP.W.1 is a copy of Erasmus's *Opus epistolarum* produced in Basel in 1529. On its title page, in a contemporary hand, is the note, "Coll. Corp.Chri Cant. / Aug.6. 1622." (Plate 11) The date August 6 gives a hint of its significance, for that (which was Matthew Parker's birthday) was the one appointed for the annual book audit. Following this idea into the College accounts for 1622 I find the item, "To Mr Greene for Erasmus epist. in fol. for ye vpper Liberarie vijs." (Plate 12) In other words, despite its early printing date nearly fifty years before

Parker's death, this copy is not a Parker book but a replacement for a Parker book lost through supine negligence. In effect it supplies the second item in the section *Rethorica* (p. 32), "ffarrago epistolarum Erasmi" of 1519.

Another case is the two-volume edition of Bullinger's commentary on the Gospels, printed in Zurich in 1546 (E.4.8, E.4.17, Register, p. 14). The bindings of these two volumes, though both are sixteenth-century, do not match; volume two has a roll-stamped calf binding, but volume one is in stamped white pigskin, presumably German. The College accounts explain this difference, for they show that the first volume is a replacement of a book reported lost in 1608. In that year the accounts include an entry, "To Burwell the stationer for the first part of Bullinger supèr Evangelia, to supplie the want in the, 3:Classis, of the outward librarie iiijs." Sixty years after the original edition was printed the Fellows of Corpus were able to get a copy of its first volume to make up for the one they had supinely lost.

A number of such replacements are recorded in the College's accounts, though they do not always include full details of the books. However, a close examination of the accounts for the seventeenth century would certainly add considerably to our knowledge of the history of the Parker collection and give an idea of how conscientiously it was audited. From a comparatively modest year such as 1603 when they record, 'Item books bought for / the inward library / Hippocrates iijs iiijd / Fulgetius de memorabilibus ijs iiijd' to the bumper year of 1607 when the auditors clobbered the College for the replacement of twelve books at the cost of 26*s* 11*d*.

The examples I have quoted are insidious since the replacement volumes were printed before the year of Parker's death, 1575. Had we not got the reference in the accounts, or some similar piece of evidence, we would have no clear confirmation that they were not part of Parker's personal library. Sometimes, of course, a replacement volume is clearly a replacement. The Register (p. 79) has the item "Archandam &c of phisniognomye 8 1530" among the books in parchment closures. This book was reported missing in 1600 and cost 8*d* to replace. The replacement volume is the English translation, *The most excellent, profitable and pleasant booke, of the famous doctor and expert astrologian, Arcandam or Aleandrin* . . . (=SP 451) published in London in 1598, and so it cannot possibly be one of Matthew Parker's books. It is certainly in a parchment closure, but one of unusual style for Parker, making use of an old page from a service book.

In defining Parker's printed books we face a problem like that posed by the Markaunt bequest for the manuscripts. There is a similar bequest from Peter Nobys, who was Master of Corpus Christi from 1516 to 1523 when he resigned and vanished from College records and apparently also from universal history. In his will Nobys left the College a considerable library whose details were recently rediscovered by Mrs. Catherine Hall on the dorse of a copy of his testament in the College archives (XXXI.128). (Plate 13) It catalogues 188 items. A few are described as *in scripto* or some similar phrase, but I do not know if we are entitled to assume from this that books not so described were printed. It would seem logical to do so. It is unfortunate that Nobys did not define his books with the sort of precision that Markaunt's executors used, or indeed with the details that Parker's Register provides. Instead he gives general titles, with occasionally a note of the number of volumes in a set or the general size. As:

> Item opera beati Bernardi in vno magno
> Item summa predicantium broymrard (*sic*, for "bromyard") in duobus
> Item Beda super epistolas pauli
> Item ludulphus de vita christi
> Item quinquagena augustini
> Item cathena aurea et homilie super euangelia.

When Parker became Master of Corpus Christi in 1544 the books of the Nobys bequest "were found to be much out of order," whatever that may mean (Masters 1753:62). He instructed the keepers to take greater care of them. What then happened to the books is unknown, since only rarely is it possible to identify with certainty one of Nobys's on the present library shelves. One such is SP 142, *Nicolaus de Orbellis super sententias* printed for Jean Petit of Paris some time between 1503 and 1515. This is Nobys no.137, "Dorbellus super sententias" (Gaselee 228). A note in Parker's hand on fol. 1^{v} asserts that the marginalia of this volume are in Nobys's hand. The title page has the ownership mark "Liber collegij corporisx."

This formula seems to indicate a distinction between books belonging to the College proper and those of the Parker bequest. This can be demonstrated by the two copies of the 1515 edition of Berthorius's *Morale reductorium* (Gaselee 175, 176). One was among Matthew Parker's books, listed as "Moralitates Bartholij 1 vol. fo. lig. 1515" among the items of *Theologica postremæ ætatis*. Peter Nobys also had a copy, entered as "Moralisationes Biblie," no. 19 of his list. Both survive in the library, as EP.T.4 and 5. What makes it clear that it is EP.T.4 that is the Nobys copy is that its fore-edge title, "Berthorii / Moralizaciones," agrees with the Nobys catalogue entry and that it has in a sixteenth-century hand the ownership inscription "Liber collegij corporis Christi" on the title page and the first page of gathering *b*. EP.T.5 has no such inscription and is apparently Parker's.

The two volumes I have mentioned as being from Nobys's library are differently treated in the sixteenth century: the *Morale reductorium* was not incorporated into Parker's collection, perhaps because Parker already had a copy; the Nicolaus de Orbellis was listed in Parker's Register, on p. 86 where it is given the printing date 1540. The date is of course wrong, but it is the date written in a Parkerian hand on the volume's title page.

From this it is clear that the Parker Register may include, among its printed books, books that were already in the College, perhaps from Nobys's bequest, perhaps from other sources. Thus it is wise to suspect all early copies of books, say from pre-1525, that are in both the Nobys and Parker catalogues. Sometimes it can be clearly shown that a Nobys book did *not* get sucked into the Parker collection: as, for example, Nobys's copy of Valerius Maximus's anecdotes from classical history (no. 17), which is the present EP.R.8, published in Paris c.1517 (Gaselee 208). Parker never claimed to own this work, and Nobys's own copy must be that recorded in the catalogue of *libri dati ab alijs* which fills an original blank (p. 37) in the Register.

On the other hand, when both Nobys and Parker claim to have a copy of *Destructorium viciorum* (Nobys no. 50, Parker Register p. 9.13 giving the date 1521—there was a French edition that year), we may justly wonder if these two entries refer to the same or to different books. Only one copy survives in the later records, and we cannot check from the present shelves because *Destructorium viciorum* was one of the books lost in 1607. It was replaced by an incunable, EP.E.11, at a cost of 6*s* 6*d*.

Of course, one must not jump too readily to the suspicion that Parker "borrowed" Nobys's books. To take an example. The Parker Register lists (p. 10.9) a copy of the *Revelationes* of St. Birgitta with the date 1492 which looks suspiciously early for him. Nobys also lists a copy (no. 45). Luckily both early examples survive in the present library, showing that the 1492 one was certainly Parker's (EP.C.10, Gaselee 38). Nobys had the slightly later edition of 1500 (EP.V.9). On the first page of its gathering *b* it has written "liber collegij corporis christi," and on the title page the variant "Benet colege Boke," distinguishing it from Parker's. (Plate 14) Yet that Parker did occasionally take books from Nobys's bequest and incorporate them into his own collection can be proven and may often be suspected.

By now my bemused readers will be wondering if there is anything certain one can say about Parker's own collection. Are there any books which can, without any doubt, be ascribed to Parker? Of course there are, a considerable and impressive number and on a wide range of topics, for he was indeed "a mighty Collector of Books." There are certainly many books which Parker, in his own lifetime, publicly proclaimed as his: those where the bindings show his initials—personal (MP) or episcopal (MC)—or his device—the key and star derived from his arms (Plates 15a, b, and 16); those which he signed with his own hand or put his monogram on (Plates 17a, b, and 18); books sponsored by Parker, and presumably, those with extensive annotations in his own hand; or books he received as presents, such as the Christmas gift of MS CCCC 24 on whose flyleaf he wrote "Hic liber datus Mattheo / Cantuar per D. A. p[er]ne 20 december 1567."

There are also books that can properly be traced through Parker though they were not originally his. An example is EP.G.3, a copy of Boccaccio's *De genealogia deorum* printed in Venice in 1492 (Gaselee 43–44) On p. 1 is an inscription which ascribes it to the College of Stoke-by-Clare, of which Parker was Dean until its suppression in 1547. (Plate 19) The perquisites of the college went to Sir John Cheke, Parker's friend, and it is reasonable to assume that Parker took over this volume (as apparently he took over a small panel of painted glass which he brought to Corpus) *in memoriam* (Masters 1753:80).

Parker was also a colleague and friend of the Alsatian reformer Martin Bucer, who became Regius Professor of Divinity at Cambridge in 1550 and died the following year. Parker preached the memorial sermon, *Howe we ought to take the death of the godly*, and acted as Bucer's executor. It is not surprising, therefore, that several of Bucer's own books are in Parker's collection. They can be identified by Bucer's name or initials in the volume or stamped on the binding, or by his virtually unintelligible hand in notes within the book (he himself was to lament the *imbecillitas* of his script), or by some similar evidence. As the rather sad entry inside the cover of his copy of the *Carmina* of Gregory Nazanzenus (SP 332): this simply says, "Sum Martini Buceri" (I am Martin Bucer's) to which is added "fui" (well, I was). (Plate 20) Or the slip of paper found between the leaves of a copy of Hermann of Wied's *Von Gottes Gnaden*, printed in Bonn in 1543 (SP 303), which is a receipt in Parker's hand for three pounds (? of bullion) to be converted into English currency: it is made out in the name of Martin Breme who was Bucer's amanuensis.

In this lecture I have tried to show not just that Parker was the great bibliophile that Strype described, but also something of the range of books, written and printed, he collected and, though this is much less clear, something of how he collected them. There will always be questions. Numbers of his books have the names of other owners or users on the title page or elsewhere within. These names can sometimes be identified, sometimes not. Sometimes the identification is uninteresting, as if it turns out to be that of a Fellow of Corpus Christi post-1575 who wrote in one of Parker's books despite the archbishop's stern injunctions. Not only Fellows either, for in 1588 one George Bulwer signed his name in EP.H.8, Johannes Mesue, *Opera medicinalia* of 1495 (Gaselee 59), and he was only a pensioner, which suggests that Parker's regulations were being liberally interpreted within a few years of his death. Sometimes we know nothing of the identity of a man who annotated a book. Who was Steven Bordworthe? He wrote "thys ys M doctor steuyn Bordworthe Boke" on fol. 2^r and asked for the reader's prayers on the final page of EP.E.8, a copy of Albertus de Eyb's *Margarita poetica* bound with Cicero's *Epistolae ad familiares*, both printed in Paris in 1477 and bound together in a late fifteenth-century binding (Weale 1894–98:R302). Who was the Thomas Coobe who paid 6*s* for and wrote his name, later erased, on the title page of EP.E.14, a composite volume made up of Isidore's *Etymologiae*, Johannes de Sacro Bosco's *Sphaera mundi*, and Laurentius Valle's *Elegantiae*? Was he in fact the Thomas Cobbe who was a Fellow of Corpus Christi 1531–44 (Gaselee 99)?

Occasionally we can trace something of the way a book came to Parker. The two parts of *Summa summarum que Silvestrina dicitur* published in Lyon in 1519 (SP 341 and 263, now SP 341A, B) were the property of Thomas Yale who signed both title pages. Then he gave the books away, for volume 1 has on its title page "Ex dono Doctoris Yale / Anno 1559° Janua 5°. NR." and the name "Nico. / Roby." in the title-page device. The same hand wrote "Nic.Roby [. . .] / ex dono / Doctoris Yale" in volume 2. (Plates 21 and 22) We can trace both these. They were men from the Queens' College, Cambridge, of the 1540s. Yale became a cleric and ecclesiastical lawyer, one of those called upon to confirm the validity of Parker's consecration in 1559. The recipient of his Twelfth Night gift was Nicolas Robinson who became the reforming Bishop of Bangor in 1566. Both were close to Parker, Robinson at one time his chaplain. As bishop he corresponded with Parker and sent him material on early records in Wales. Presumably from him Parker got this pair of volumes.

There remain puzzles. Parker had a copy of the 1535 edition of Vegetius, *De re militari* (SP 311). Some thirty years after its publication this copy came into the hands of one of Parker's coadjutors, who signs the final page: "Stephanus Batmanus me possidet." He adds the date, 1568 and price, 3*s* 4*d*. (Plate 23) A few years later this volume appears in Parker's Register of Books (p. 75) and not in a position that suggests it was a recent addition to the collection. Did Batman buy it on Parker's instructions? That seems unlikely in view of the firm statement of the inscription. Did Parker covet and eventually possess Batman's second-hand bargain? If so, on what conditions?

Again, Parker had a copy of the splendid 1570 edition of Ortelius's *Theatrum orbis terrarum* (EP.Q.16), and his name, in italic script and in its episcopal style, "Mathew Cantuar," is on the opening flyleaf. Before this, however, there is bound into the volume a slip of paper with, in red crayon, John Parker's name, the price 40*s*., and the date, probably 1572 but perhaps 1571—the final digit is uncertain. This book also occurs in the Parker Register (p. 74) but at the end of a list, which indeed suggests a late acquisition. Did John buy it on his father's behalf with the inserted slip recording how much Matthew owed him? Or is there another story behind this?

But this is enough in general terms of Parker's collection of books. In my next lecture I look at a particular aspect of the collection, Parker's historical interests and his publishing ventures based upon them: his attempt at "the conseruation of . . . auncient recordes and monumentes."

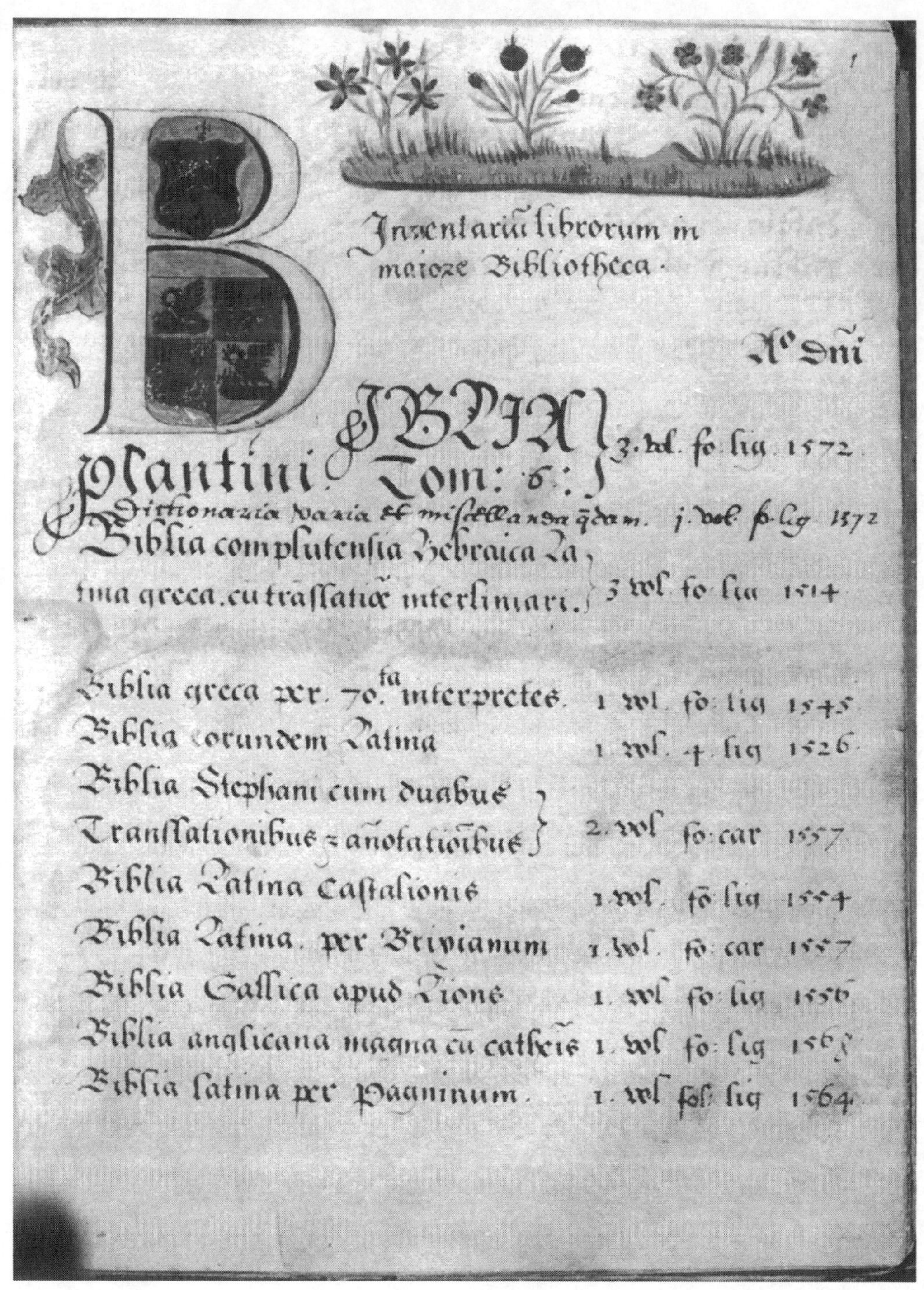

1

Inventariū librorum in maiore Bibliotheca.

Aᵒ Dñi

BIBLIA Plantini Tom: 6: } 3. vol. fo. lig. 1572

Dictionaria varia et miscellanea quedam. j. vol. fo. lig. 1572

Biblia complutensia Hebraica Latina greca. cū trāslatiōe interliniari. } 3 vol. fo. lig. 1514

Biblia greca per 70.ta interpretes. 1 vol. fo. lig. 1545

Biblia eorundem Latina 1. vol. 4. lig. 1526

Biblia Stephani cum duabus Translationibus & añotatiōibus } 2. vol fo. car 1557

Biblia Latina Castalionis 1. vol. fo. lig 1554

Biblia Latina per Brixianum 1. vol. fo. car 1557

Biblia Gallica apud Lions 1. vol fo. lig 1556

Biblia anglicana magna cū cathcis 1. vol fo: lig 1568

Biblia latina per Pagninum. 1. vol fol: lig 1564

Plate 1 MS CCCC 575, p. 1: The opening of the inventory of Matthew Parker's books in the Corpus Christi College version of the Parker Register

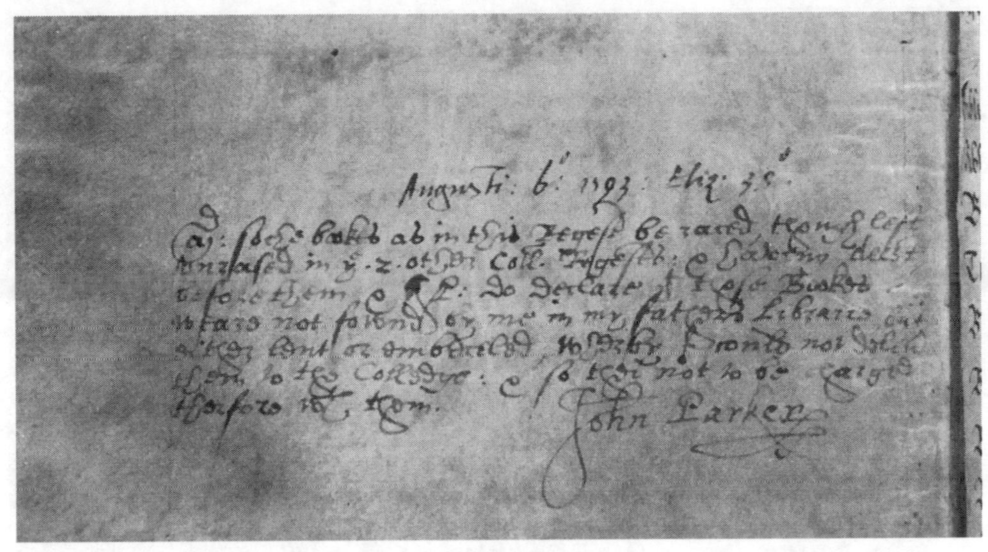

Augusti: 6: 1593: Eliz: 35

John Parker

Plate 2 MS CCCC 575, p. xxii: John Parker's declaration of the authority of his corrections to the Parker Register lists (6 August 1593)

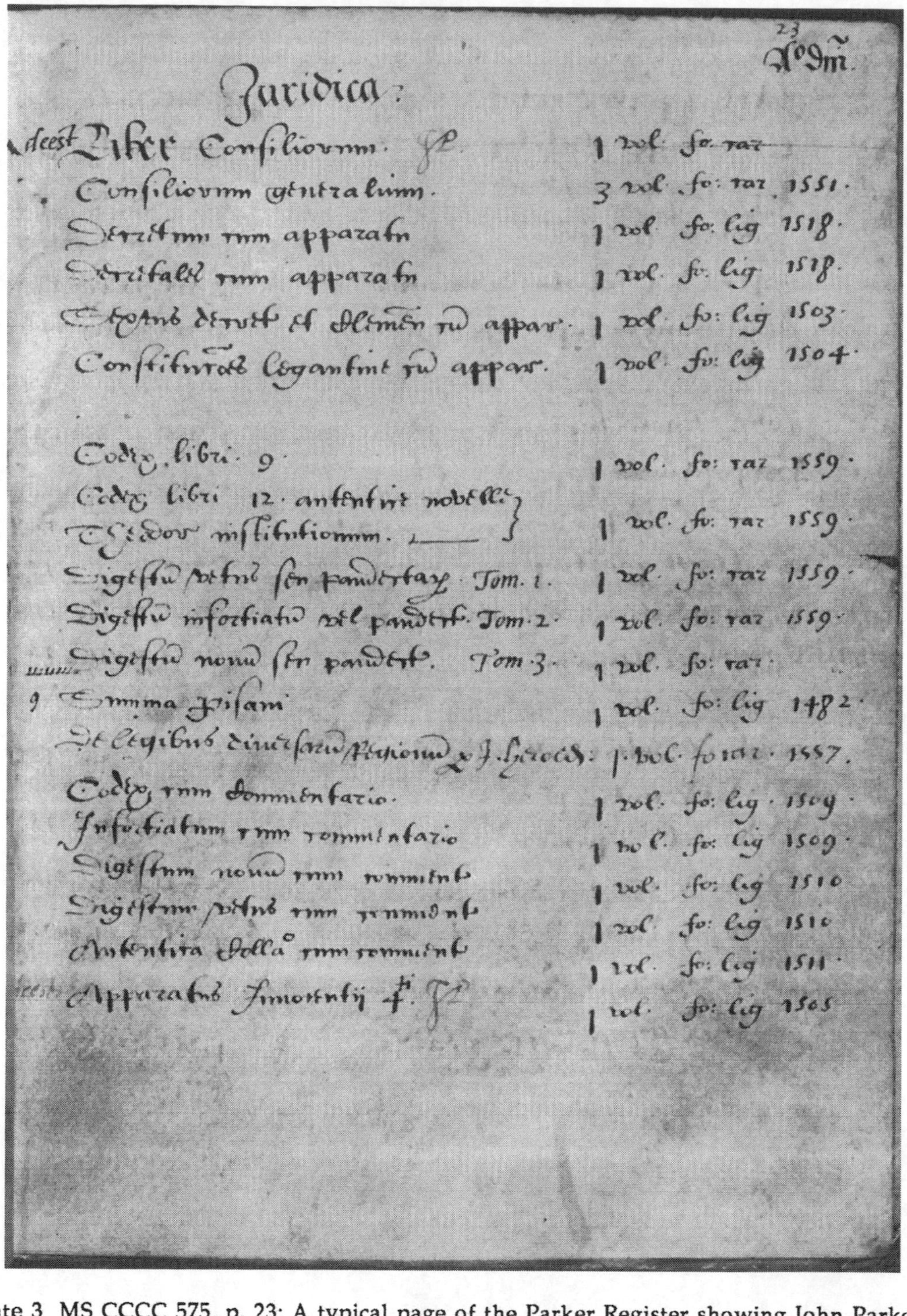
23
A° 9m.

Juridica:

deest Liber Conciliorum. 1 vol. fo. rar

Conciliorum generalium. 3 vol. fo: rar 1551.

Decretum cum apparatu 1 vol. fo: lig 1518.

Decretales cum apparatu 1 vol. fo: lig 1518.

Sextus decretalium et Clementinae cum appar. 1 vol. fo: lig 1503.

Constitutiones legantinae cum appar. 1 vol. fo: lig 1504.

Codex, libri 9. 1 vol. fo: rar 1559.

Codex libri 12. autentica novellae / et eorum institutionum. 1 vol. fo: rar 1559.

Digestum vetus seu pandectarum. Tom. 1. 1 vol. fo: rar 1559.

Digestum infortiatum vel pandect. Tom. 2. 1 vol. fo: rar 1559.

Digestum novum seu pandect. Tom. 3. 1 vol. fo: rar

9 Summa pisani 1 vol. fo: lig 1482.

De legibus diversarum regionum per J. Herold. 1 vol. fo rar 1557.

Codex cum commentario. 1 vol. fo: lig 1509.

Infortiatum cum commentario 1 vol. fo: lig 1509.

Digestum novum cum comment. 1 vol. fo: lig 1510

Digestum vetus cum comment. 1 vol. fo: lig 1510

Autentica volla° cum comment. 1 vol. fo: lig 1511

deest Apparatus Innocentii 4ti. 1 vol. fo: lig 1505

Plate 3 MS CCCC 575, p. 23: A typical page of the Parker Register showing John Parker's annotations and, in the left margin, an added numeral showing the beginning of a new press mark (9)

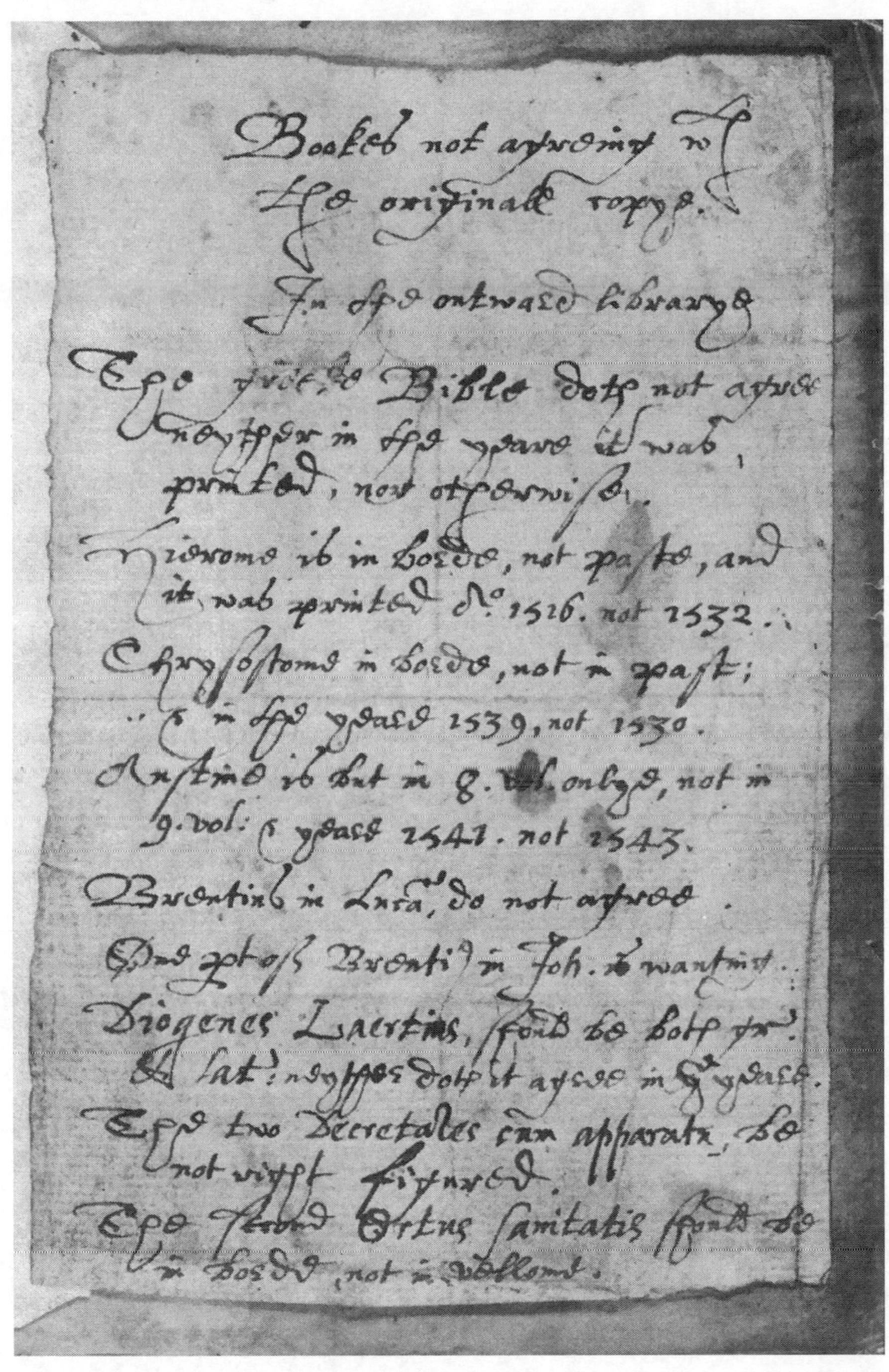

Bookes not agreeing w[ith] the originall copye.

In the outward librarye

The great Bible doth not agree neyther in the yeare it was printed, nor otherwise.

Hierome is in borde, not paste, and it was printed A[o]. 1526. not 1532.

Chrysostome in borde, not in past; & in the yeare 1539, not 1530.

Austine is but in 8. vol. onlye, not in 9. vol: & yeare 1541. not 1543.

Brentius in Luca, do not agree.

One tome of Brentius in Joh. is wanting.

Diogenes Laertius, should be both gr: & lat: neyther doth it agree in the yeare.

The two Decretales cum apparatu, be not with figured.

The second Ortus sanitatis should be in borde, not in vellome.

Plate 4 MS CCCC 575, recto of front endpaper: An added list of corrections of "Bookes not agreeing with the originall copye"

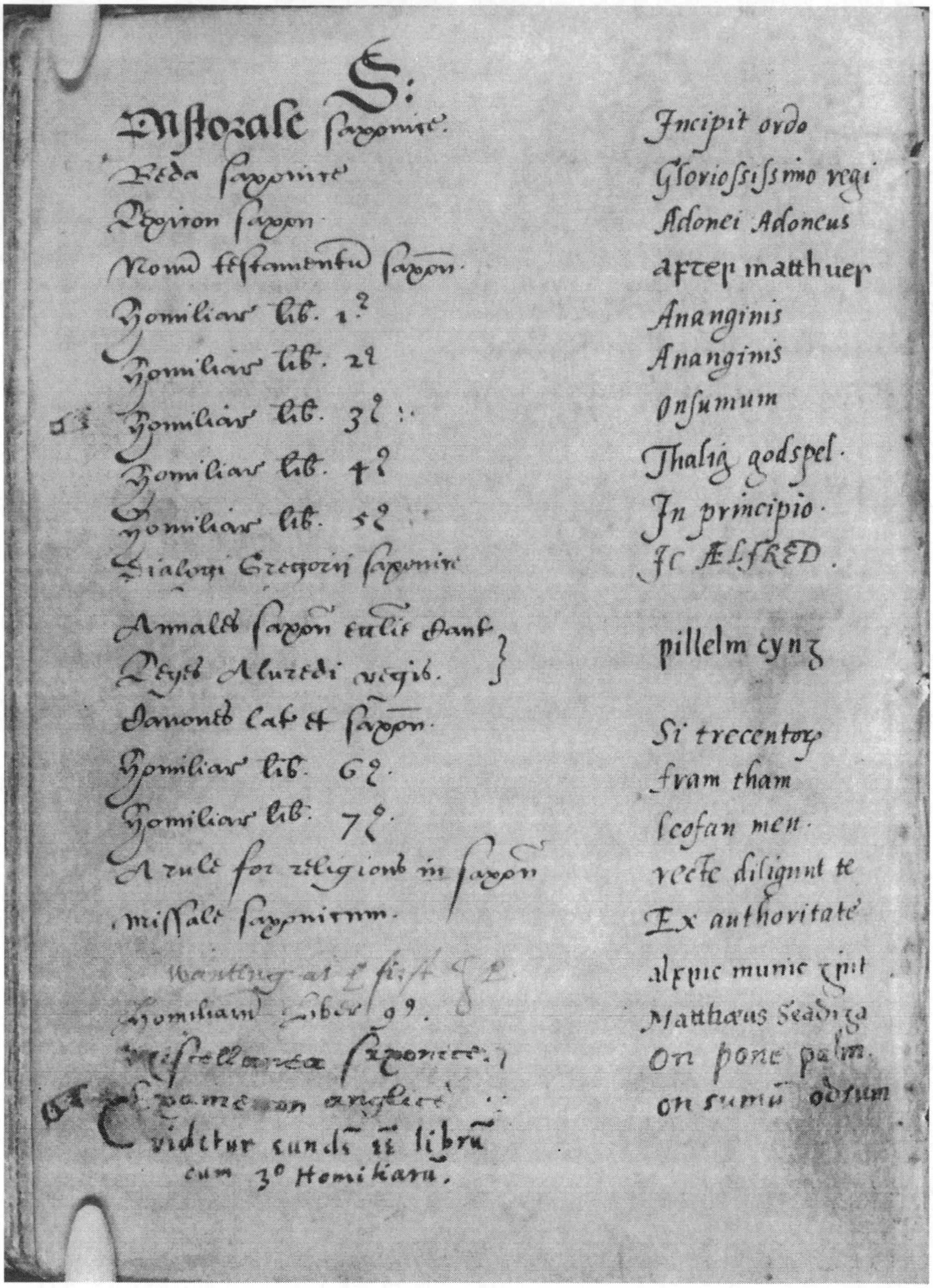

Plate 5 MS CCCC 575, p. 62: A list of manuscripts in section S of the Parker Register, including the Parker text of the *Anglo-Saxon Chronicle* which is the eleventh item on the list

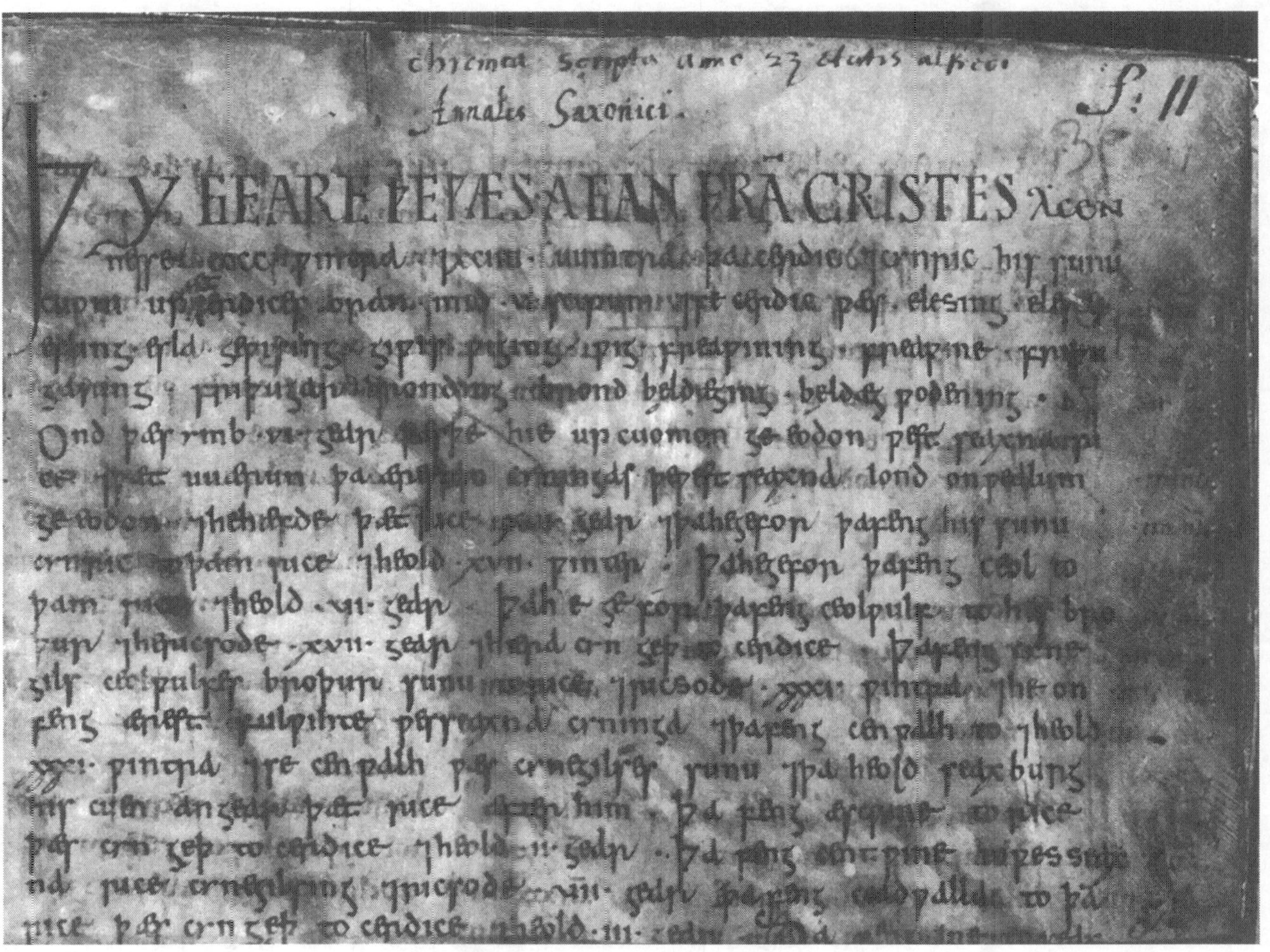

Plate 6 MS CCCC 173, fol. 1r: The present opening page of the Parker *Chronicle* with (?) Parker's added title (reduced)

Plate 7 MS CCCC 197B, fol. 1^{r}: St. John's eagle—the present opening page of a collection of Gospel Book fragments with Parker's comment in the top margin (reduced)

Plate 8 MS CCCC 41, p. 1: The opening of the Old English translation of Bede's *Ecclesiastical History* with added ownership inscription (reduced)

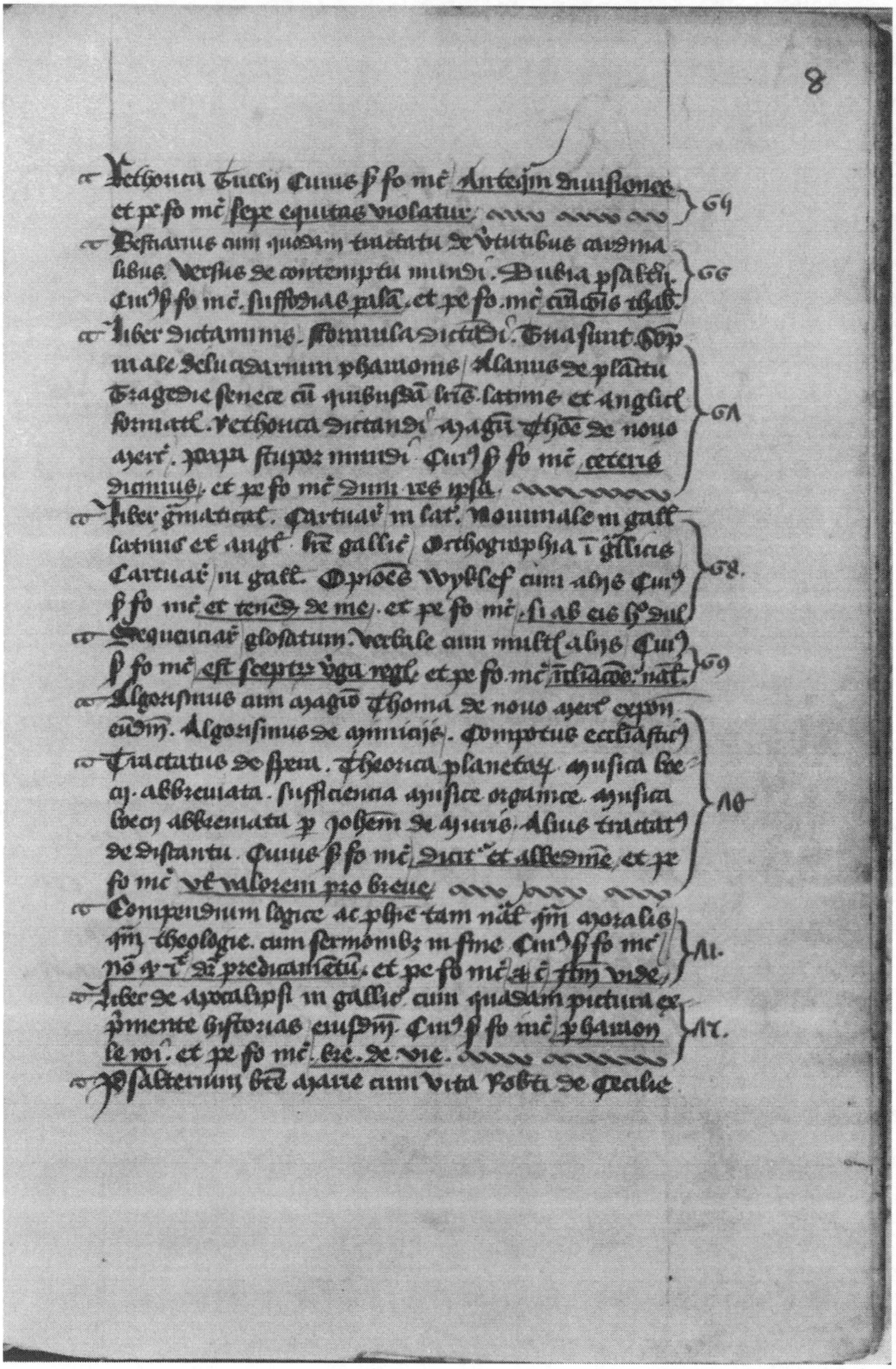

Plate 9 MS CCCC 232, fol. 8r: A page from the inventory of Thomas Markaunt's books (reduced)

1. Orō Jo: Boxolli.
25. Epta cuiusdam Angli.
39. Of the soueraigntie of England
167. Of Cokery and seruing of meates.
201. An epistle of the Dukes mariage.
211. A discourse of the same.
225. An oratiō of the Recorder of London.
243. Catalogus eorū qui scripserunt in Biblia.
267. The bourning of Paules.
283. A treatise for housholders.
311. Ane admonition to the lordis of Scotland.
343. An edict of the French King
391. A disclosing of the bull.
411. An answere to the Portugall pearle.

Plate 10 The flyleaf of printed book SP 447: A list of fourteen individual items

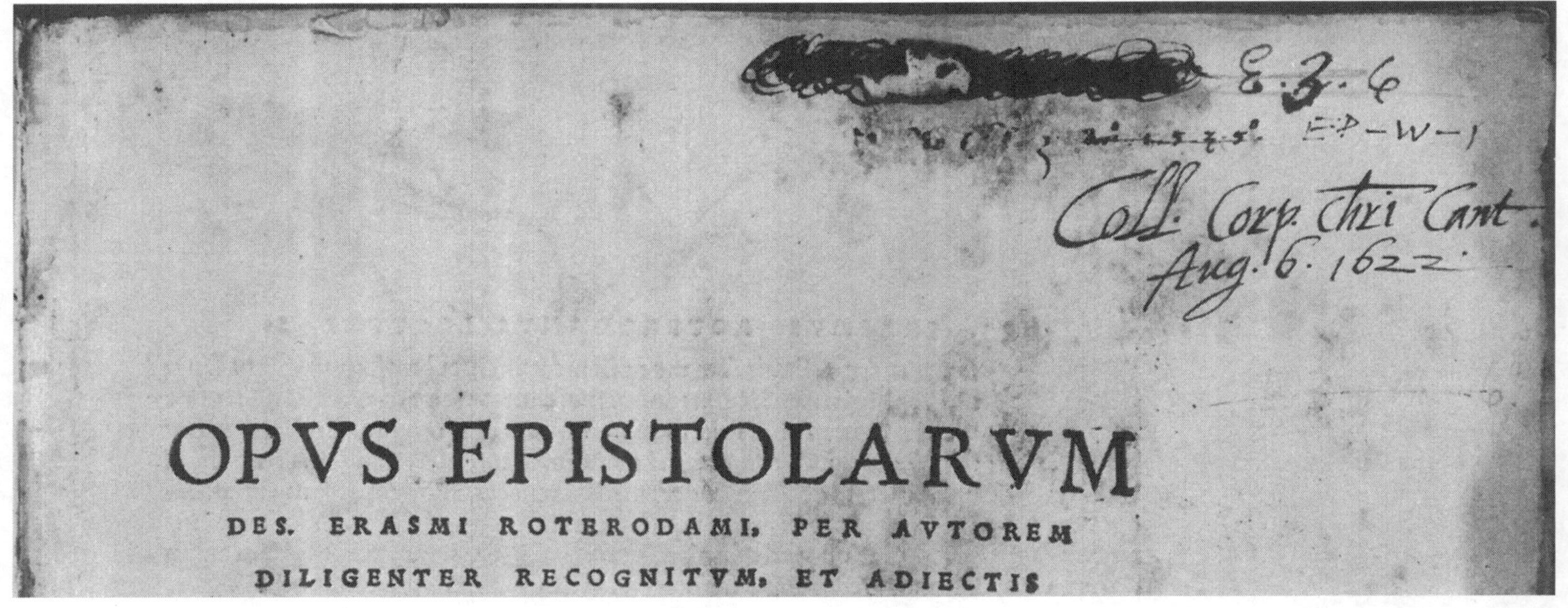

Plate 11 The dating note on the title page of printed book EP.W.1 (reduced)

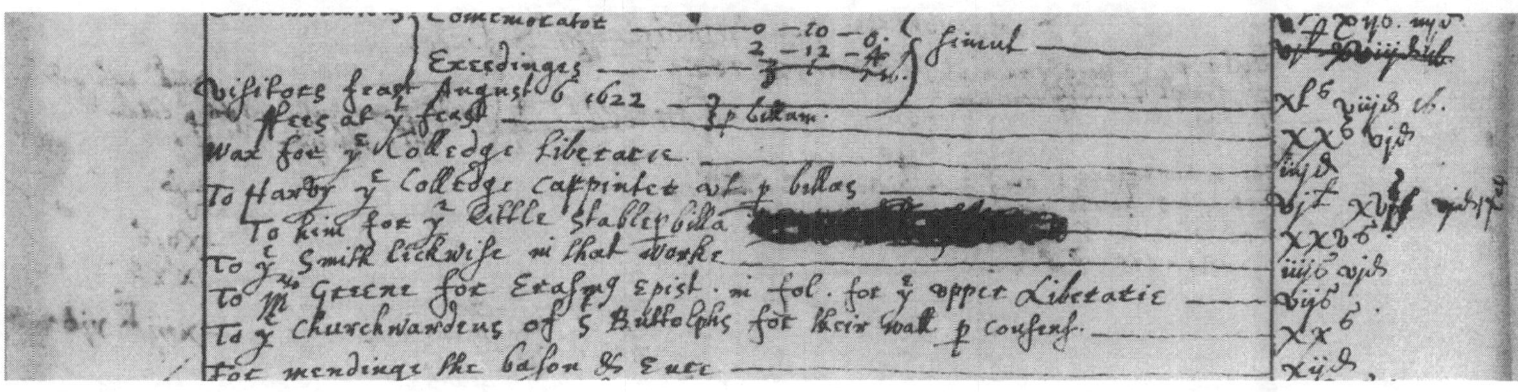

Plate 12 The entry in the College accounts recording the purchase of printed book EP.W.1 (reduced)

Plate 13 CCCC Archives XXXI.128 (dorse): Part of the list of books left to the College by Peter Nobys (reduced)

Plate 14 The title page of printed book EP.V.9: The inscription shows that the book belonged to Benet, i.e., Corpus Christi, College (reduced)

a.

b.

Plate 15 Printed book M.2.4: a) back cover, Matthew Parker's personal initials used as ownershp inscription; b) front cover, Matthew Parker's episcopal initials used as ownership inscription (reduced)

Plate 16 Back cover of printed book G.3.7: Matthew Parker's device of star and key deriving from his personal arms (reduced)

a.

b.

Plate 17 Title pages of printed books: a) E.5.14, Matthew Parker's signature used as ownership inscription; b) B.4.16, Matthew Parker's initials (reduced)

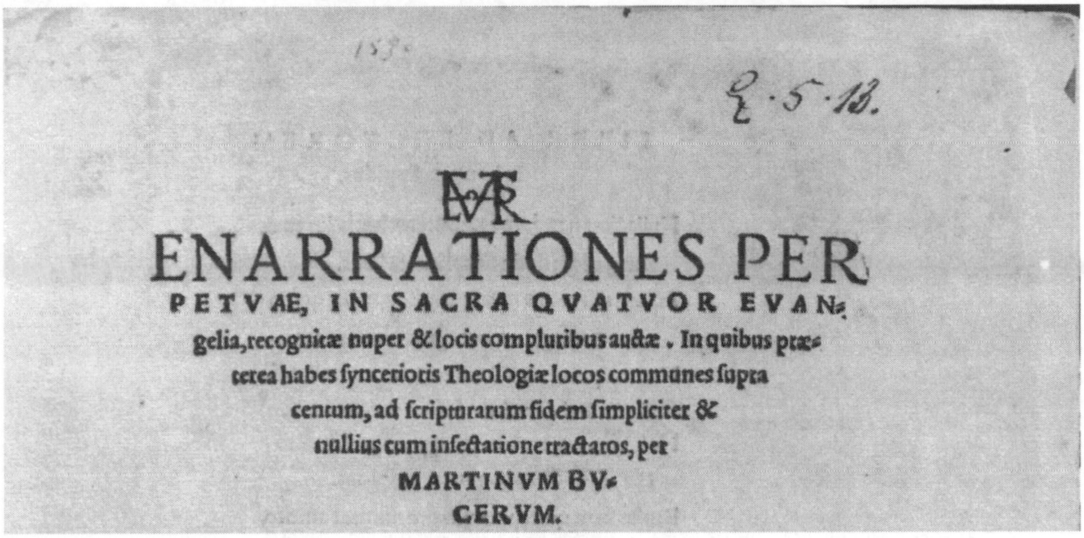

E.5.13.

ENARRATIONES PERPETVAE, IN SACRA QVATVOR EVANGELIA, recognitæ nuper & locis compluribus auctæ. In quibus prætetea habes synceritoris Theologiæ locos communes supra centum, ad scripturarum fidem simpliciter & nullius cum insectatione tractatos, per MARTINVM BVCERVM.

Plate 18 Title page of printed book E.5.13: Matthew Parker's monogram used as ownership inscription

Liber collegij de Stoke iuxta clare

Genealogię deorũ gentlium Ioannis Bocacii de certaldo ad Vgonem inclytum Hierusalem & Cypri regem.eiusdem libri prohoemium.

S Atis ex relatis Donini Parmēsis egregii militis tui.uera percepi Rex inclyte sũmopere cupis Genealogiam deorũ

Plate 19 Printed book EP.G.3, fol. 1r: Ownership inscription of the College of Stoke-by-Clare (reduced)

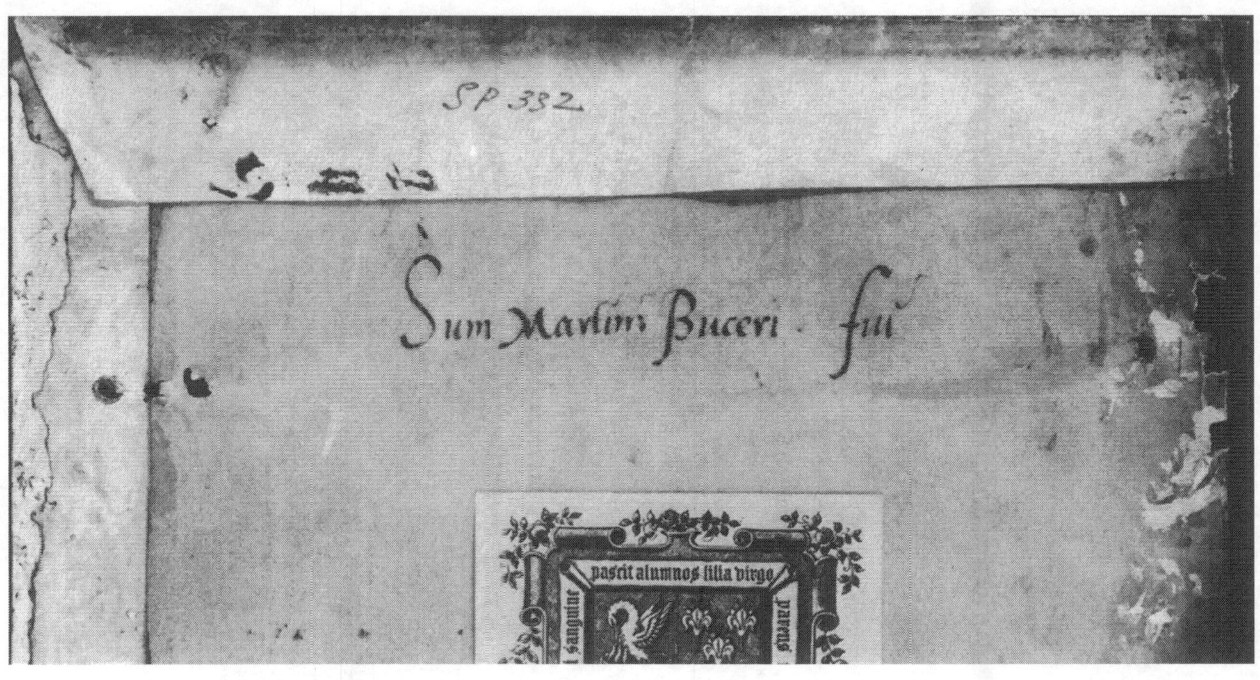

Plate 20 Inside front cover of printed book SP 332: Record of Martin Bucer's ownership

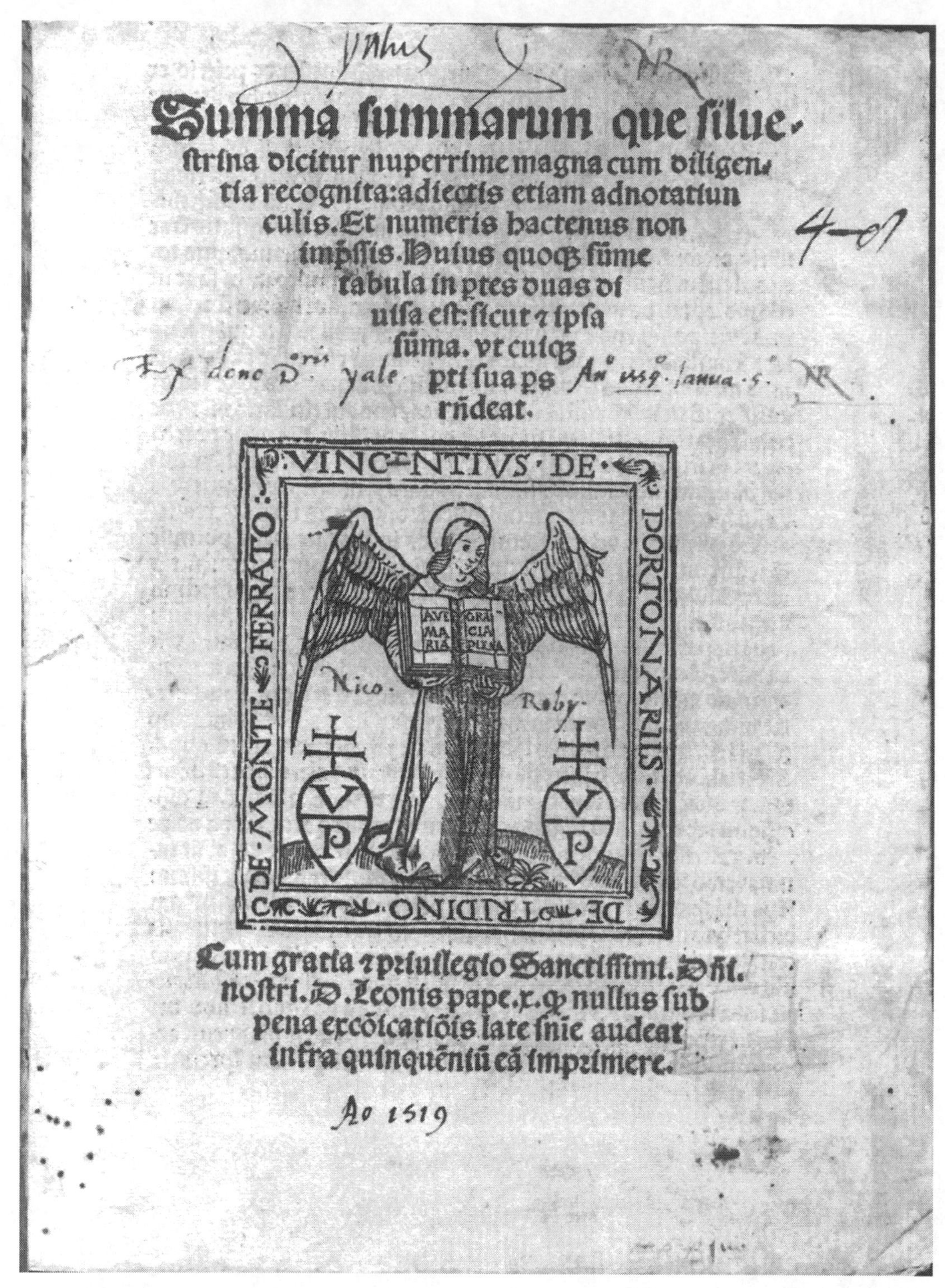

Summa summarum que silue-
strina dicitur nuperrime magna cum diligentia recognita: adiectis etiam adnotatiun
culis. Et numeris hactenus non
impssis. Huius quoq3 sūme
tabula in ptes duas di
uisa est: sicut & ipsa
sūma. vt cuiq3
pti sua ps
rñdeat.

Cum gratia & priuilegio Sanctissimi. Dñi.
nostri. D. Leonis pape. x. q nullus sub
pena excōicatiōis late snie audeat
infra quinquēniū eā imprimere.

Plate 21 Title page of printed book SP 341A: Inscription records gift from Thomas Yale to Nicolas Robinson (reduced)

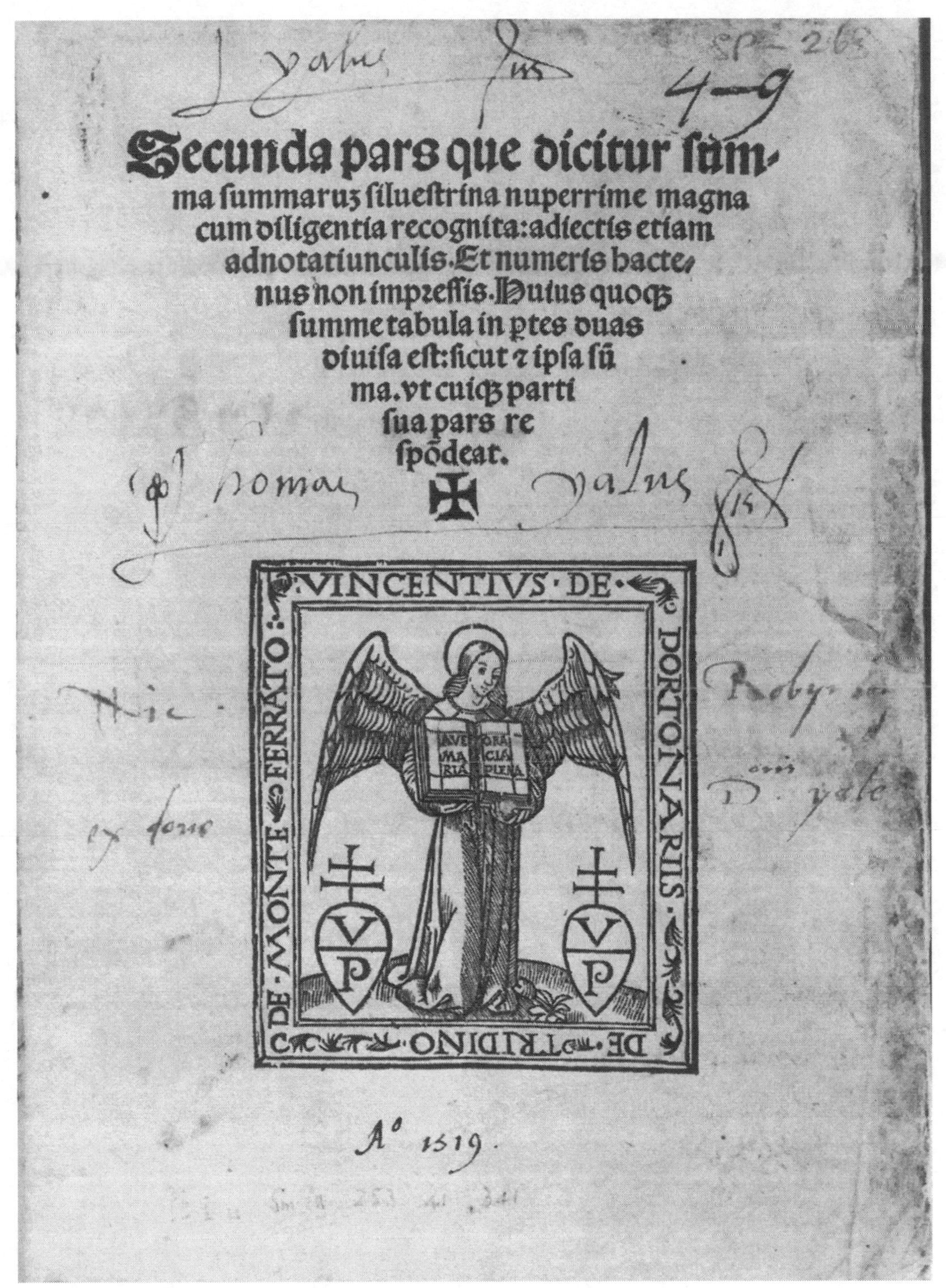

Secunda pars que dicitur ſum-
ma ſummaruʒ ſilueſtrina nuperrime magna
cum diligentia recognita: adiectis etiam
adnotatiunculis. Et numeris hactenus non impreſſis. Huius quoqꝫ
ſumme tabula in ꝑtes duas
diuiſa eſt: ſicut ⁊ ipſa ſū
ma. vt cuiqꝫ parti
ſua pars re
ſpōdeat.

Plate 22 Title page of printed book SP 341B: Inscription records gift from Thomas Yale to Nicolas Robinson (reduced)

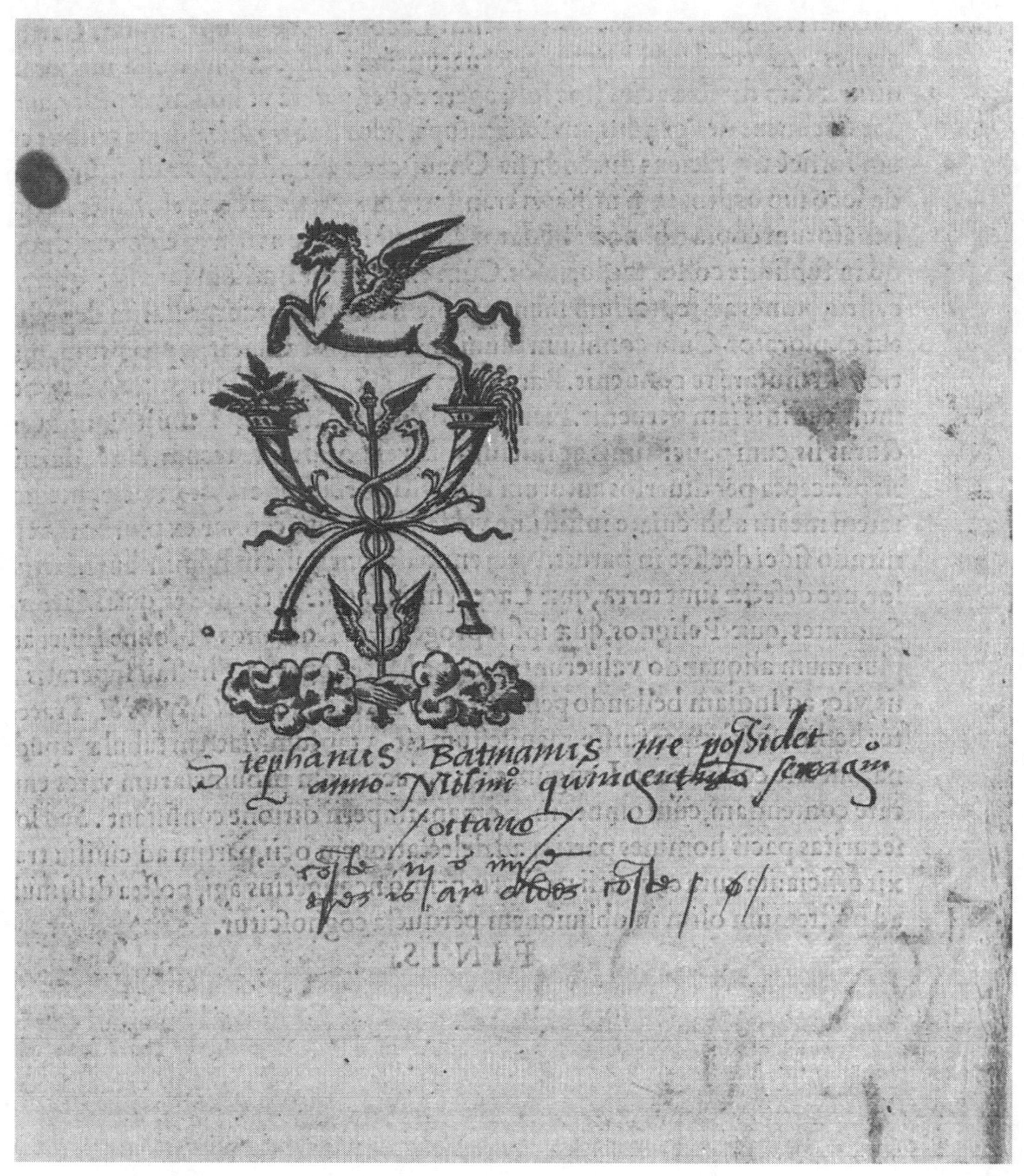

Plate 23 Printed book SP 311, p. 280: Stephen Batman's record of purchase (reduced)

THE CONSERVATION OF ANCIENT RECORDS AND MONUMENTS

When John Strype defined Matthew Parker as "a mighty Collector of Books," he added Parker's reason for making his collection: "to preserve, as much as could be, the antient Monuments of the learned Men of our Nation from perishing." But the classic statement of Parker's intent is in a broadsheet issued on the authority of the Privy Council and dated 7 July 1568 (STC 7754.6). (Plate 24) This dwelt on the care which—following the lead her predecessors had given—Queen Elizabeth had shown for "the conseruation of such auncient recordes and monumentes, written of the state and affaires of these her realmes of Englande and Irelande." Such historical manuscripts "heretofore were preserued and recorded by speciall appoyntment of certaine of her auncetours, in diuers Abbeyes, to be as treasure houses, to kepe and leaue in memorie such occurrentes as fell in their tymes." Now, continues the broadsheet, these records have passed into private hands and so are little known despite their manifest historical testimony. The Council then addresses a request "to all and singuler her subiectes within her Realme of Englande" directing owners of such "auncient recordes or monumentes written," on the receipt of a summons from the Archbishop of Canterbury, to "gently impart the same" to him,

> Not meanyng hereby in thuse of such bookes for a tyme, to withdrawe them from your ryght & interest vnto them, but after a tyme of perusyng of the same, vpon promis or bande, to make restitution of them agayne safely into your handes.

There they would remain until needed for study or collation in connection with any dispute about "the antiquitie of the state of these countryes."

Here Parker got his orders, though it is only fair to admit that he asked for them in a letter dated 4 July [1568] to Sir William Cecil (Bruce and Perowne 1853:327). Parker was to constitute, as it were, a one-man Royal Commission on Historical Manuscripts: he was to collect them together, to study and presumably record them, and then to send them back. The first two parts of this task he accomplished admirably. How many of the books that remained in Parker's hands came to him through this commission I do not know. Certainly Parker was collecting manuscripts well before 1568 as his correspondence shows. Presumably this was the continuation of a fever for books that had raged in him for many years. In 1563, for instance, he was negotiating for Cranmer's papers (Bruce and Perowne 1853:186–87, 191–92). His Bucer manuscripts apparently came to him at the reformer's death in 1551. His volume with the ownership mark of the College of Stoke-by-Clare presumably on the suppression of that house in 1547. I suppose that any Corpus Christi books that were in his keeping date from the years of his Mastership, 1544–53.

As several discussions have shown (James 1899; Wright 1951), Parker got his medieval English manuscripts from a wide range of provenances. N. R. Ker's catalogue of the medieval libraries of Great Britain (Ker 1964:337–39) shows an amazing number of primary sources for them—though of course Parker may have got many through intermediaries or from secondary owners. For what it is worth Ker lists Corpus Christi manuscripts from Bury St. Edmunds, St. Albans, Worcester, Canterbury (both Christ Church and St. Augustine's), Norwich, Malmesbury, Abingdon, Exeter, Peterborough, Rochester, Sawley, Bath, Hexham, Durham, St. David's, London, Thorney, Ely, Winchester, Sherborne, Wenlock, Ramsey and many more. (Plates 25a, b, 26a, b, 27a, b) His ardor for the "conseruation of such auncient recordes and monumentes" was intense.

Conservation is a word now popular among librarians, less so among readers. Yet "conservation" properly understood should be for the ultimate benefit of both. I suppose we might define the word, bibliographically, as "treating a book in such a way as to preserve the greatest amount of evidence it contains, consistent with its being available for reading with discretion." As such conservation must have the support of all responsible library users, those who have a care not only for their own interests but for those of future scholars or scholars in other disciplines. Libraries throughout the world are becoming more and more conscious of the problems that increased numbers of research students pose, of the danger this puts documents in. To this extent they are appearing more restrictive than in the past. It is only those readers without discretion, who, sick of self-love, think their own immediate interests more important than their subject's future, who will object to such restrictions. Unfortunately there are many such readers, many in high academic position.

Parker himself was firmly restrictive in the conditions he imposed upon those who kept his library under the terms of the indenture of January 1574. He restricted access to it to the Master and Fellows of Corpus Christi and to the Masters and two Senior Fellows of Gonville and Caius and of Trinity Hall. Readers must behave themselves:

> nor should anyone write in [the books] nor stealthily remove leaves and quires from any of the same, but in the continuing course of time, in part in restoring books, in part in binding them together anew, each in his own way, as led by a pious impulse of charity, shall occupy himself in assisting the work of the libraries.

The *registrarius* of Corpus Christi—who seems to have been the library's only paid servant—should keep an eye on any outside reader—those dubious characters from the colleges across the way. He must

> take heed that none of the books standing there suffer any damage. For it is otherwise ungracious in the extreme and quite beyond all reason that those from whom you have readily accepted some profit or benefit should either be repaid with discourtesy or that the ingratitude of forgetfulness should intervene.

And would that all readers in the Parker Library would keep this thought in mind. But I digress, and "The regularity of my design / Forbids all wandering as the worst of sinning."

Strype claimed that the world should be grateful to Parker for "retrieving many antient Authors, *Saxon* and *British* as well as *Norman*, and for restoring and enlightening a great deal of the antient History of this noble Island." Like his present-day successors Parker was deeply concerned with conservation and preservation, but inevitably he interpreted this concern rather differently from us.

We who have been brought up in a printed book culture find it natural to regard a book as a complete and discrete object, a finished work. It requires something of a shift of thinking to see it as a collection of quires that could be added to or subtracted from, that would be at risk if the binding structure collapsed or the sewing broke. Yet it is clear that in many, perhaps most, cases Parker's "auncient recordes or monumentes written" were in a shaky state. Moreover, as I showed in my last lecture, Parker made the practice of binding together separate and sometimes incongruous manuscripts, adding material or moving it round, repaginating a composite volume. Is this conservation? The interventions of sixteenth-century owners are a major aspect of manuscript history. Parker's deserve some investigation.

Parker was an orderly man. He liked a book to open and close neatly. Hence he would alter the beginning or the last leaves of a manuscript to tidy it up. In my last lecture we saw this happening to CCCC MS 173 part 1, the Parker manuscript of the *Anglo-Saxon Chronicle*, where even after his red crayon pagination he seems to have removed the unnecessary first leaf and opened his *Chronicle* with a written heading added over the Alfredian genealogy of p. 3 that begins the main text. Let us see more examples of this intervention.

A disbound manuscript might easily lose opening or closing quire or leaves. What was left might then begin with the last part of a text whose opening was lost, or close with the beginning of a text which had no ending. Parker did not like this and cleared it away. An example is CCCC 44, a splendid Anglo-Saxon pontifical. Two leaves are missing from its first quire. This contained at least two Anglo-Saxon texts, practically all the first now lost. The present p. 1 has been washed out, but there can just be traced the remains of a text on the first four lines which has not been identified. The last sixteen lines of the page held part of a translation of the *Liber officialis* of Amalarius (Trahern 1973). Parker wrote his name in red crayon at the top of the washed-out page and also annotated the manuscript elsewhere, so it was presumably he who was responsible for cleaning off the first side to give a neat opening rather than a messy fragment of Old English. (Plate 28)

CCCC 9 now has as its opening a calendar, with the beginning of its main text, a passional, on p. 17. Immediately before this one or more quires are missing. The end of the preceding text, which occupied the opening lines of the first column of p. 17, has been erased so that the manuscript now begins coherently. What now constitutes the opening, *Cristo igitur*, is recorded as the *incipit* of this volume in the Parker Register of Books.

Again, CCCC 303, a book of Old English homilies, has lost its opening sections. The pages still hold traces of a (?) late medieval folio numbering in pencil in the center of the top margin, now often ploughed away. There is also a sixteenth-century ink page number at the outer top corner of each recto. As far as one can read it, the medieval numbering is forty-four leaves above the sixteenth-century: that is, by the later date forty-four leaves had disappeared from the front of the manuscript. The sixteenth-century contents list makes use of the medieval numbering, which was probably therefore more completely visible than it now is, and its first item is fol. 45. It looks as though the cropping of the upper edge of these leaves post-dates this contents list, and may be Parkerian or may be later, since the volume was rebound in the eighteenth century. On the present p. 1 a strip of parchment was stuck to the very top: on it is written the book's title, "Homiliarum saxonicarum Li. 9us," with part of the title of the existing first item also copied in in a sixteenth-century hand. When this parchment was lifted it was found to hide the remains of the last four lines of a preceding item, covered up because it was an untidy end of a lost text. (Plates 29 and 30)

CCCC 188 presents a more complex case. It is defective at both beginning and end. At the bottom of the present final folio is the title SERMO DE DIE IUDICII followed by two lines of text that have been washed out. In contrast, the defect at the beginning has been supplied, presumably by a Parkerian scribe, imitating an Anglo-Saxon hand. The first surviving page of the original manuscript had been given the page number 1; thereafter, a new opening leaf was added to contain the missing material, and the numbering was then changed so that 1 was replaced by 3.

Adding supply material at the beginning, at the end, or interpolated in the middle of a manuscript was a common Parkerian practice. To this end, as we know, his household contained several scribes trained to imitate, with greater or lesser success, earlier and medieval styles of calligraphy. Typical examples of Parkerian supply additions are:

(1) The opening of CCCC 449, a defective copy of Ælfric's *Grammar* and *Glossary* dating from the eleventh century. In this case the missing material was copied in from a manuscript that is now British Library MS, Royal 15 B xxii. (Plate 31) As I have already pointed out, this Royal manuscript had been in Parker's hands in the sixteenth century, and it contains some of his red crayon annotation. Here there is strong presumptive evidence of Parker's direction to his scribes to complete a defective manuscript from an alternative text he had access to. Indeed he—or someone within his circle—marked red crayon slashes in the Royal text to indicate where CCCC 449 now began.

(2) Lost quires in CCCC 383, a legal miscellany from shortly after the Norman Conquest and deriving ultimately from St. Paul's, London. This was apparently unbound when Parker received it, so some quires were missing. Material was supplied from British Library MS, Harley 55 to make up for this loss. (Plate 32) I do not know if Harley 55 was ever formally in Parker's possession, but he certainly annotated it, adding headings to the laws and red crayon numbering and underlining.

I have illustrated some curious examples of Parker's conservation, which clearly also included (as I hope modern conservation does not) destruction of what he thought expendable and we would think valuable. So far I have pointed to examples where clear traces of his destructive activity are still visible. There are also cases where we can deduce this destructive activity but not demonstrate it. An example is CCCC 196. This is a large fragment of the Old English *Martyrology*, apparently from eleventh-century Exeter. It now begins on a new page, part-way through the entry for 19 March in a quire that wants its first leaf. It has no heading, no Parkerian pagination or contents list. The present opening words, *se ys to þam*, are those recorded in the *incipit* of the Parker Register. Yet we can have some idea of what was lost. In 1974 Günther Kotzor pointed out that in his *Collectanea*—British Library MS, Cotton Vitellius D. vii—John Joscelyn copied a passage from the entry for 17 March which must have come from CCCC 196 (Kotzor 1974). Such a passage would have been on the leaf that immediately preceded the present first one, presumably therefore the opening leaf of the quire. The present front page is in poor condition, and it may well be that the volume was long disbound and that the preceding leaf became badly torn, did not protect its following leaf well, and eventually was lost. It may have been cut away since the conjoint leaf now shows a clean cut rather than a tear (though it is hard to see because of the tightness of the binding), but that could also be the effect of rebinding in the eighteenth or again in the twentieth century. At any rate, in the mid sixteenth century the quire's opening page was still extant and apparently still part of the volume. Joscelyn became Parker's Latin secretary in 1559 when Matthew become Archbishop of Canterbury. Sometime between then and the date of drafting of the Parker Register list this leaf had been removed.

Another sort of destruction affected CCCC 197B, the Anglo-Saxon Gospel Book fragment discussed above. This was bound up with other manuscripts, some of them paper, some time in the sixteenth century, so forming the composite CCCC 197. Since the paper was much smaller than the Gospel Book, the latter was drastically cut down to bring it to a comparable size. This cropped some of the decoration on the opening display page of St. John's Gospel, now fol. 2^{r}, (Plate 33) and also cut severely into the margins of the text pages, occasionally clipping parts of the text. (Plate 34) The Parkerian red crayon page numbering, which follows the composite manuscript, is squeezed into the space available on the cut-down page; usually it is just above the first written line of the text, but sometimes so little space was available that it had to be fitted in between first and second text lines. I do not see any connection between the material of the Gospel Book and the contents of the manuscripts that were bound to it, so the cutting down of this magnificent codex seems to us a wanton act for which Parker must be held responsible.

The curious may then ask the question: what happened to such pieces of vellum as were cut away. One answer is illustrated by CCCC

557. (Plate 35) Though this is grandiloquently called a manuscript it is in fact only two small fragments of an Old English text on the history of the true cross, otherwise known in a twelfth-century version. They were found some decades ago during rebinding of two printed books that belonged to Parker: (1) SP 4, two parts of Johannes Carion's *Chronicon* published in 1563 and 1568 respectively, bound together in a single volume that has a stamped leather binding with two roll stamps not precisely recorded in Oldham 1952; and (2) SP 260, *De fide Iesu et Iesuitarum . . .* , published in 1573, in a stiff parchment binding with no special characteristics. These two volumes are recorded on a single leaf of the Parker Register of Books (pp. 97–98) which, from its rather unusual form, looks like one designed to contain a number of late additions to Parker's collection, so the two bindings can be ascribed to the very end of Parker's career, perhaps 1574 or 1575. Parker had his own binders and may have supplied them with binding parchment from what he had cut out of manuscripts or salvaged from fragmentary materials. These two bits of Old English manuscript, by the same scribe, come from Worcester, as is shown by their annotations in a well-known thirteenth-century hand known romantically to Middle English philologists as the "tremulous Worcester hand." SP 4's companion volume (SP 210), books 1–3 of Carion's *Chronicon*, has a matching binding but its binding strips are, alas, only sixteenth-century while a further volume (SP 30) using the same stamps, published in 1573, has later medieval ones. It seems it was a matter of chance what bit of parchment the binder picked up for any volume.

We have seen how Parker made the opening of a volume look neat by removing unattractive features. Another way was by adding an attractive opening page. I begin with two manuscripts that follow in sequence in the present manuscript numbering: CCCC 162 and 163. These were distant in the arrangement of the Parker Register, S.5 and I.3 respectively. Presumably it was the eighteenth-century martinet librarian James Nasmith—"a Scot by origin and a drill-sergeant by temperament"—who created the present number system of cataloguing and who put these two in sequence, thinking them similar in appearance.

CCCC 162 has an added group of fly-leaves, at the end of which is a woodcut of the crucifixion; stuck to its back is a Parkerian list of the contents of the manuscript, a collection of Anglo-Saxon homilies. (Plate

36) The woodcut, on parchment, is taken from a missal, probably one printed in Paris in the 1520s or 1530s (closely related to STC 16205, 16214). With light shining through the page from the back it becomes clear that this is the verso of a leaf Bii of such a book, and with more research it should be possible to identify the issue with certainty. The added frontispiece of CCCC 163, an eleventh-century service book, has a similar effect. Again it is a woodcut, but a more primitive one. This time it is English work closely related to, but not identical with, the crucifixion picture used by Richard Pynson for his Sarum Missal of 1512 (STC 16190). In these two cases Parker was apparently cutting up printed books which were no longer acceptable to the reformed church of the 1560s or 1570s, and so were expendable.

However, what are we to say to the openings of two manuscripts, CCCC 419 and CCCC 452 (Plate 37), unrelated to one another, though closely similar in size? The first is an eleventh-century book of vernacular homilies, the second a twelfth-century text of Eadmer's *Historia novorum*. To each of them Parker added an opening picture which Ker identified as "taken from the same thirteenth-century psalter" (Ker 1957:116). The same psalter, thinks Ker, provided the pictures added to the MacDurnan Gospels, now Lambeth Palace Library, MS 771, and on this evidence attributes the latter to Parker's collection (Ker 1957:346–47). The pictures that form the frontispieces to CCCC 419 and 452 have no connection with the texts and are added solely for adornment. The odd thing is that CCCC 419 has a twin homily book, now CCCC 421. This too had a frontispiece added, and it is a little surprising that, if Parker plundered a psalter for CCCC 419, he did not do the same for CCCC 421. In fact Parker seems to have plundered CCCC 419 to make an opening picture for CCCC 421, for the latter now begins with a crucifixion scene which Ker thinks once formed the first leaf of CCCC 419. It seems that Parker had no clearly defined plan for his interventions in manuscripts.

One of Parker's letters provides the *locus classicus* for illustrating his habit of adding a decorative page to the opening of a manuscript. Writing to Sir William Cecil in January 1565/66 and returning a manuscript that he had borrowed from him Parker says:

> I retorne to youe your boke agayn. . . . I had thought to have made up the want of the begynnyng of the psalter. for yt wanteth the first psalme and III

> verses in the second psalme: and me thought the leafe goyng before the XXVI psalme wold have ben a mete begynnyng before the holl psalter. having david sitting with his harpe or psaltery dechacordo vel ogdochordo with his mynistres with ther tubis ductilibus, et cymbalis sonoris etc and then the first psalme wryten on the backe side; which I was in mynd to have caused Lylye to have counterfeted in antiquitie etc but that I called to remembrance that ye have a synguler artificer to adorne the same which your honor shal do wel to have the monument fynyshed, or ellys I wil cause yt to be done and remytted agayn to your library (Wright 1967:36).

Here are familiar aspects of Parker's treatment of manuscripts: moving a page from one place to another to form "a mete begynnyng"; writing on the verso to fill in a gap in the text; and imitating an earlier script form. So common was this to Parker that he was prepared to apply it to someone else's book.

Here we return to the general question of conservation and preservation of records and monuments written. Certainly Parker was eager to preserve a large amount of early material. We must watch with admiration the progress of his collection, the efforts he made to secure it, and the detailed study of manuscripts that he made, as I shall show later. But side by side with conserving, Parker was destroying. By using the psalter pictures for CCCC 419 and 452 he certainly enhanced—at least in his own opinion—the appearance of those manuscripts; but what did he do to the psalter he plundered? Of course, the psalter would have been a Popish one, in a tongue not understanded of the people, and so not conformable to contemporary Protestant usage. It may have been fragmentary or at least imperfect (as apparently was the Gospel Book, CCCC 197B, when Parker received it). It is easy enough to sympathize with Parker's attitude. Yet we have to admit that in improving some books he damaged others. And he certainly removed parts of some texts that he thought intrusive or ugly. Like the wild West Wind he was both "destroyer and preserver."

The case of CCCC 198 brings forward a new type of evidence. This volume, Parker's fourth book of homilies, opens with a frontispiece, an eleventh-century colored line drawing. It is an addition, and possibly a Parkerian addition though not certainly so (Ker 1957:76). The evidence in favor of Parkerian intervention here is: (a) the verso of the drawing was used for the contents list of the manuscript, written directly on the parchment rather than on an added paper slip as is more common; and (b) the end of the manuscript is tidied up. The contents list records a final homily, *De virginitate*, on fol. 395. The codex now ends with fol. 394, the penultimate folio of a quire of ten that lacks its tenth leaf. Thus the homily was lost after the contents list was drawn up. It seems, however, that its opening was in fact at the bottom of fol. 394^v, for there five lines of text have been erased, leaving only traces of a capital. In other words, the manuscript has been given a Parkerian good ending. It seems most probable that he gave it also a good beginning.

This example shows the importance of the contents lists that in Parker's time were attached to the openings of many of his books. They often record a manuscript state earlier than that now preserved and so name texts that have vanished since the mid sixteenth century. It is unfortunate that, as I suspect, some of these lists were thrown aside by the eighteenth-century rebinders of some of the Corpus manuscripts: see Nasmith's remarks quoted earlier.

Revealing is the sixteenth-century contents list of CCCC 178. This codex is now a composite one; its first part an eleventh-century Old English homily book, its second a Latin-Old English version of the Rule of St. Benedict. Both come from Worcester for they are glossed in the "tremulous hand"; though they were not necessarily bound together in their Worcester days. The contents list gives, first, the thirty-one homilies of part one; two are out of order, originally missed out and added at the end. Thus the last two in terms of page order are nos. 28 and 29 in the Parkerian count, *In die pentecostes* (fol. 263) and *De septiformi spiritu* (fol. 274). There follows a gap in the contents list and then is named *Regula d.Benedicti/cum capitibus.71.*, beginning on fol. 287. (Plate 38)

In fact the list is in error here, for these are pages not folios—CCCC 178 is paginated throughout in Parkerian red crayon. The list makes it clear that there is a lacuna in the first part, which now ends at p. 270, though part two begins, as the list indicates, at p. 287. Thus sixteen pages/eight folios, presumably a single quire containing the end of *In die pentecostes* and all of *De septiformi spiritu*, have been lost at some stage, and this loss postdates the Parkerian page numbering and the combining of the two manuscripts. There is no evidence exactly when. The manuscript was taken out for rebinding in 1748 in a group of some two dozen manuscripts, and returned five days later—an enviable record of productivity. By that date the quire was already missing, for the 1722 printed catalogue of the Corpus manuscripts records the loss: "Homiliarum Saxonicarum liber secundus, sive viginti novem Homiliæ in linguâ Saxonicâ. Desunt duæ, quarum in Indice fit mentio. Saltem una & pars alteræ excisa" (The second book of homilies, or twenty-nine homilies in the Anglo-Saxon language. Two mentioned in the index are missing. At any rate one and part of a second have been cut out [Stanley 1722:56]). The two missing homilies were obviously those of the lost quire.

There is clear evidence that this manuscript was disbound in Parkerian times. The third item in its list of homilies is *Interrogatio Sigiuulfi*, and for this no folio/page numbering is supplied. The reason for this is that the item is no longer in CCCC 178, and was presumably missing when the folio/page numbers were filled in on the contents list, though presumably it was there when the list was being planned. There is no corresponding gap in the red crayon numbering on the pages of the manuscript, so the *Interrogatio* had gone before that took place.

What happened is that one whole item, the *Interrogatio*, was taken from CCCC 178 and placed in CCCC 162. This not only involved disbinding both manuscripts, but also required cutting the quires of CCCC 178 since the eleven leaves that held the item belonged to three separate quires. Since the *Interrogatio* both began and ended halfway down a page, CCCC 178 lost the last half-page of the preceding item and the first half-page of the following. (Plate 39) To fill this gap in CCCC 178 a single new leaf was written out, which copied these two text fragments in an imitation of Old English script. This was inserted into CCCC 178. (Plate 40) To identify the writer of these copies would be difficult in view of our ignorance of the "Old English" hands of sixteenth-century scribes. Luckily the two texts had been glossed by the tremulous Worcester scribe, and the copyist added some of the Worcester glosses in his texts, this time using his own script. And his own script makes it clear—at any rate to me—that this is Parker himself. So here we have a clear picture of Matthew mutilating one manuscript by transferring pages to another. Why, I have not the slightest idea.

There is a last bizarre twist to the story. CCCC 178 has a final parchment flyleaf reusing a contemporary legal document. On its back is written, in Parkerian red crayon, "Summa tota paginarum 580"; the number is altered from or to 570, then crossed out and corrected to 568. The flyleaf is numbered on its verso 562, again in Parkerian crayon, but the final leaf of CCCC 178 proper is only 457/58. What happened to the hundred or so missing pages? Why is the total number given as 568 or thereabouts? The answer is a simple one: this flyleaf is now in the wrong manuscript. It properly belongs to CCCC 162 whose last numbered leaf is 569/[70]. At some stage in their history these two manuscripts were disbound simultaneously, and the flyleaf was rebound into the wrong one. Such a disbinding must have happened in Parkerian times, otherwise the *Interrogatio* could not have been moved from one to the other. Could the flyleaf error have happened at any other time also? Well, CCCC 178 was rebound in 1748; unfortunately, so was CCCC 162, and in the same batch as CCCC 178. (Plate 41) So the switch of flyleaves could have taken place at that date.

Hitherto I have spoken mainly of Matthew Parker's treatment of Anglo-Saxon manuscripts, and there is no doubt that in so doing I have slanted my argument. It is fairly clear that it was the Anglo-Saxon materials that attracted the archbishop's attention during his last decades (as I shall show next lecture), and that in consequence they were more profoundly affected than others. But the 1568 broadsheet was more general in its application, speaking of "auncient recordes and monumentes"; and the bulk of material of this sort would be from the later Middle Ages, from the twelfth century and after. Here too it is clear that Parker not only collected manuscripts but used them: reading, cross-referencing, and commenting upon them. For instance, the twelfth-century historian Eadmer was one of Parker's favorites, as we shall see when we come to the use he made of his major manuscript of the *Historia novorum*. When faced with other Eadmer manuscripts, Parker annotated: on the flyleaf of his book of Eadmer's extracts from the work of Archbishop Anselm (CCCC 457) he wrote, "Edmerus author/is qui scripsit historiam/rerum novarum in anglia" (Plate 42); faced with the preface of Eadmer's *Life of Anselm* (CCCC 318) he would add a cross-reference to the *Historia novorum*; at the beginning of a collection of minor Eadmer works (CCCC 371) he gives that author a date, "Edmerus vixit anno 1121."

In fact Parker collected together many of the standard primary sources of history or of pseudo-history—Henry of Huntingdon, William of Malmesbury, Geoffrey of Monmouth, Symeon of Durham, and a whole range of minor chroniclers and local antiquaries. In addition he commanded a considerable number of copies of manuscripts in the possession of other collectors, as the Rochester Chronicle that now forms British Library MS, Cotton Nero D ii, copied as CCCC 342. There is a complete subject here that I have not time to include in my lectures; instead, I want to discuss what use Parker made of some of these materials.

Lambeth Palace MS 959 is a copy of the printed book *De antiquitate Britannicæ Ecclesiæ* interleaved with manuscript material, much of it Parkerian. This book deserves a study of its own. Fol. 369[v] contains a list of books published in the time of (and apparently under the supervision of) Matthew Parker, with a special group marked out as completed "at the (?) gages of" the archbishop. The list, twenty-nine items in all, is very varied, and includes some items that may not have been published, in our sense of the word, at all. This includes broadsheets and ephemera as well as books. Some of the items I have not identified. Titles are often heavily abbreviated, and in the account below I expand abbreviations silently. The list opens with:

(1) *Bibliorum sacrorum translatio et recognitio in magno Volumine cum Tabulis et prefationibus*, or as we would call it, the Bishop's Bible of 1568. Many of the other entries can be grouped under subject matter.

(2) Several works on the practices, principles, discipline, and history of the Anglican church; such as *De Antiquitate Britannicæ ecclesiæ cum .70. Archiepiscopis Cantuariensibus* (STC 19292, which came out in 1572 and was reissued in many forms); *The table of Diett in Englishe* (STC 6836.5 *A Dietarie. Writtes published after the ordinaunce of earles and barons. Anno domini 1315*, a broadsheet of [?] 1570); *The Table of Degrees in mariage*, Parker's issue of the table of kindred and affinity, his own copy of which is dated 1560 (CCCC 113, item 44); *An Advertizement for Apparell*, which was not I think a mail-order catalogue but presumably STC 10026, *Aduertisments . . . partly for the apparrell of all persons ecclesiasticall, by vertue of the queenes letters* (1565 and reprints).

(3) Works connected with his old college and university, in the main deriving from that controversy on the relative ages of Oxford and Cambridge which began in 1568 and was revived briefly in 1574. John Caius was the Cambridge champion who produced his amusing but in-

accurate *De Achademia Cantabrigiensi Historia.&c. & de Collegijs* (STC 4344) anonymously in 1568, and thereafter the 1574 edition, *De antiquitate Cantebrigiæ cum historia eiusdem nuper recognita et emissa* (STC 4345), and the map engraved in brass that accompanies some editions, *Mappa opidi Cantebrigiæ in ærea tabula excisa* (Plomer 1926–27). There was also a *Historia Collegij Corporis Christi* which I suppose was Joscelyn's *Historiola*, not published in Parker's (or indeed Joscelyn's) lifetime.

(4) A group of works that dealt with religious controversy: (a) the debate about the marriage of priests: *De coniugio Sacerdotum responsio ad .d. Martinum* which we know as *A defence of priestes mariages . . .* (STC 17518), and presumably linked to this the *Collectiones de coniugis sacerdotum*. To some degree connected with this dispute are *Epigrammata varia Prosperj cum coniuge in rithmo Anglico* (STC 20444.5) and *Volusiani Epistola cum dialogo Anselmi* (STC 24872) since both these deal with the celibacy of the clergy. (b) *Homilia Saxonice de Corpore Christi* (which we know as *A testimonie of antiquitie*, STC 159 and 159.5) upon the nature of the eucharist. (c) *Evangelia Saxonicè cum prefatione* (STC 2961), the Anglo-Saxon and contemporary English versions of the Gospels with Foxe's preface, paying tribute to Parker and proclaiming that the Anglican Reformation "is no new reformation of thinges lately begonne, which were not before, but rather a reduction of the Church to the Pristine state of olde conformitie." This edition contributed to the controversy about the translation of the scriptures into a tongue understanded of the people.

(5) There is an occasional personal item such as *Conciones variæ. &c. in funere .d. M.Buceri &c* which I suppose is related to Parker's funeral sermon for his friend, *Howe we ought to take the death of the godly* (STC 19293: cf. STC 5108). Perhaps linked to it is *Scutum fidei: de resurrectione: consolacio de Morte*.

(6) Also listed are several translations in which Parker innocently tried his prentice hand at English verse. Not all of these I have traced, but where Parker's verse can be identified it is distinctly banal. Following from 4(c) above is *Psalterium totum versum, in varia metra Rithmica* (STC 2729). Of *Vpon Ecclesiastes of Salomon, with the Preface in englishe* all that survives are proof sheets of a number of lines of verse, the blank spaces on the back used for Corpus Christi College accounts (STC 2756.5). In this section should be counted again the version of Prosper's

epigrams, and I suppose—though I have not traced them—*Hymni quidam prudentij et aliorum. &c.* and *De aurea Mediocritate in rithmo anglico.* Promising, in view of Parker's achievement in poetry, is *A methode for making of (?) true englishe meter.*

(7) Finally there is a group of historical works that I want to look at in a little detail. Lambeth Palace MS 959 lists them as *Matthæi Paris historia maior* (STC 19209: 1570/71); *Matthæi Westmonasteriensis historia siue florilegus. bis impressus* (STC 17652–53: 1567, 1570); *Historia magna Tho: Walsingham cum ypodigmate Newstriæ* (STC 25004–05: 1574). Missing from this list is the fifth historical work whose publication is credited to Parker (if indeed credited is the right word considering the fierce criticism that has been made of his editorial methods). This work is *Ælfredi regis res gestæ* (STC 863), the biography of Alfred the Great compiled by Bishop Asser in 893. This was often issued with the Thomas Walsingham edition and may be thought subsumed under that title; however, the Asser seems to have been printed later than its companions, since Parker sent a copy of this work to Burghley in November 1574 (Bruce and Perowne 1853:468). Perhaps this is an indication that the Lambeth 959 list was compiled shortly before that date.

Though Parker's name does not appear on the title page or introduction of any of these historical works, they were patently admitted to be produced under his supervision. The decorative initials that open the prologues of Matthew of Westminster and Matthew Paris, the preface of Thomas Walsingham's *Historia,* and the dedicatory words of Asser's *Life* all enclose versions of Matthew Parker's achievement of arms, sometimes episcopal, sometimes personal, with his initials, either episcopal or personal in a couple of cases. (Plates 43a, b, and 44a) The *Ypodigma* has no such achievement, but its title page has a device with the opening words of Parker's motto *mundus transit [et concupiscentia eius].* (Plate 44b) There is no doubt Parker wanted his name to be associated with these works, and presumably his sentiment was that which opens the preface to Walsingham's *Historia*: "Cum nos non nobis solùm natos esse meminerim . . . sed Patriae, Parentibus, & Amicis, istam . . . historiam non uni mihi privatè retinendam, sed ad communem omnium utilitatem diuulgandam putavi (When I called to mind that we are not born for ourselves alone . . . but for our country, our parents and friends, I thought this . . . history should not be kept privately for myself only, but should be published for the common benefit of all). In other words, he was carrying out the trust laid upon him by the 1568 broadsheet in ensuring that the "wrytynges and recordes" did not "remayne obscure and unknowne."

The subject of the editorial methods Parker used is a complex one. Much has been written on it, usually to Parker's discredit, and I do not wish to open the matter again here (Madden 1866–69:xxxi–vii; Vaughan 1958:154). There is, however, one point that has not had the examination it deserves: the way he used his (or other's) manuscripts in printing his editions. The clearest example I know concerns his edition of Matthew Paris's *Historia maiora*. It has long been known that one of the books he used for his text here is that which is now CCCC 16. This is a largely autograph manuscript embellished with elegant colored line drawings, most by the author himself. We now think of it as one of our more precious and fragile codices, so we find it the more surprising that Parker let it go to Reginald Wolfe's printing house. Yet that is certainly what happened. Right through CCCC 16 there is, added in the margins, a collation of the manuscript text with that of the printed edition. In fact the manuscript was used as a copy text. Not only is the running pagination of the printed book given, but also the numbering within individual quires. So, for instance, on fol. 90^v is the marginal annotation, "530 (= running pagination)/Yy2 (= quiring)." (cf. Plate 45) Fol. 281^r has "1174/H.6," the latter standing for 4H iij verso. This cross-referencing from manuscript to printed book continues until the end of CCCC 16, p. 1175 (for the year 1254). When he had come to the end of CCCC 16 Parker began on the next volume. He did not have a medieval text of the continuation so he had one copied, CCCC 56 taken from British Library, Royal MS 14 c vii. On this the casting off begins again, until the end of the text which corresponds to the final page (1349) of the printed book.

So far I have shown there is close connection between these manuscripts and the printed work, but not that the manuscripts went to the printing house. That is evidenced by the plentiful splodges of printer's ink scattered through the pages, by thumb marks, by the outline of a wooden block placed on the page presumably to keep it flat, and so on. (Plates 46, 47) Once again Parker was preserving and spreading knowledge; once again damaging or destroying in the process. However, the further point is that if there is a defect in the editing, it is not because the full texts were not available to the printer. Nor do the manuscripts show—as far as I can see—any general annotations that reveal the editorial process. Future discussions of Parker's methods must consider, not only the nature of the texts but the evidence for printing.

In the case of Thomas Walsingham's *Historia* Parker had a fifteenth-century manuscript copy, CCCC 195. This was defective, and it was presumably Parker who had supply leaves added, copying, thinks James, College of Arms MS, Arundel 7 (James 1912:I.471). MS 195 too shows the signs of printing work that was seen on MSS 16 and 56. The collation is not as clearly visible as on those manuscripts because the collator sometimes used a dry-point or sometimes used pencil which was later rubbed out. Enough remains to show cross-checks between manuscript and printed edition similar to those in the Matthew Paris texts. There is also tell-tale printer's ink in the margins. There is the further subtlety of printed book line numbers added in the margins of this manuscript, and occasionally signs of Parker's characteristic red crayon.

What I have tried to show in this lecture is the lively concern Matthew Parker took in his manuscripts and the use he made of them. He was not simply a mighty collector of books, he was also a reader and annotator of them. He tried to convert them to the most suitable condition for the use he wanted of them. Inevitably much of what I have said sounds very critical. I have accused Parker of mutilating books, destroying textual material, scribbling in precious and artistically important manuscripts, and putting them at risk in various ways. This is only to say that Parker's attitude to conservation is not ours. He did not seek to preserve the same sort of evidence. There is nothing strange in that. The eighteenth century had different standards again, as is shown by its wholesale rebinding of the Corpus manuscripts. The nineteenth again, otherwise we would not have books disfigured by the reagents applied to make faded texts more easily readable. In the late nineteenth century, the Librarian, Parker's successor, took CCCC 173 out into Senate House yard and had it photographed in the sunlight there. The then Master of the College, learning of this too late, stigmatized it as "most improper." Yet we now commonly allow our manuscripts to be photographed—much research would come to an end if we did not—and from the point of view of exposure to light and of handling this too could be thought to be most improper. Each age fixes its own methods and standards of preservation, and I do not expect that the efforts we are making in the 1990s will prove any freer from criticism when we reach the early decades of the twenty-first century.

12. 49

Hereas the Queenes maieſtie, hauyng lyke care and zeale as diuers of her progenitours haue had before tymes for the conſeruation of ſuch auncient recordes and monumentes, written of the ſtate and affaires of theſe her realmes of Englande and Irelande, which heretofore were preſerued and recorded by ſpeciall appoyntment of certaine of her auncetours, in diuers Abbeyes, to be as treaſure houſes, to kepe and leaue in memorie ſuch occurrentes as fell in their tymes. And for that moſt of the ſame wrytynges and recordes ſo kept in the Monaſteries, are nowe come to the poſſeſſion of ſundry priuate perſons, and ſo partly remayne obſcure and vnknowne: in which ſayde recordes be mentioned ſuch hiſtoricall matters and monumentes of antiquitie, both for the ſtate eccleſiaſticall and ciuile gouernement. Whereypon we of the Queenes maieſties priuie counſell knowing her expreſſe pleaſure in the ſame, haue thought good to write theſe our letters to all and ſinguler her ſubiectes within her Realme of Englande, to notifie her pleaſure: which is, that the moſt reuerende father in God, and our very good lorde, the Archbiſhop of Canterbury, ſhoulde haue a ſpeciall care and ouerſyght in theſe matters aforeſayde. And therypon we wyll and require you, that when the ſayd Archbiſhop ſhall ſende his letters, or any of his learned deputies, hauyng theſe our letters, and requeſtyng to haue the ſyght of any ſuch auncient recordes or monumentes written, beyng in your cuſtodie, that you woulde at the contemplation of theſe our letters, gently impart the ſame: Not meanyng hereby in thuſe of ſuch bookes for a tyme, to withdrawe them from your ryght & intereſt vnto them, but after a tyme of peruſyng of the ſame, vpon promiſe or bande, to make reſtitution of them agayne ſafely into your handes, to be ſafely kept hereafter, ſo as both when any neede ſhall require, reſort may be made for the teſtimonie that may be founde in them, and alſo by conference of them, the antiquitie of the ſtate of theſe countryes may be reſtored to the knowledge of the world. In which your doyng ye ſhall not only ſhewe your ſelfe gratefull ſubiectes to the Queenes maieſtie your naturall prince: but alſo ſhall miniſter frendly occaſion to vs to geue you thankes, as oportunitie ſhall ſerue, in any of your cauſes, as may ryſe vpon the report of the ſayde Archbiſhop. And thus we byd you well to fare. From Howard place the ſeuenth of July. 1568.

N. Bacon C.S. T. Norffolke. VV. Northt.
R. Leyceſter. VV. Howard.
VV. Cecyll.

Facta collatione huius ſcripti cum originali, in cuſtodia ſupraſcripti Reuerendiſſimi patris exiſtente, per me Iohannem Incent, notarium publicum, eiuſdem Reuerendiſſimi patris Regiſtrarium principalem, concordat cum eadem.

Plate 24 The Privy Council broadsheet of 1568, MS CCCC 114 p. 49 (reduced)

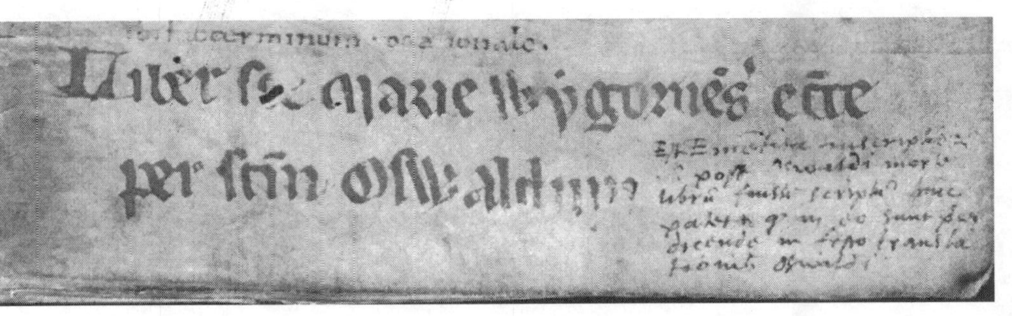

a.

b.

Plate 25 Former ownership marks of Corpus Christi manuscripts from (a) Worcester and (b) Malmesbury

a.

b.

Plate 26 Former ownership marks of Corpus Christi manuscripts from (a) Rochester and (b) Christ Church, Canterbury

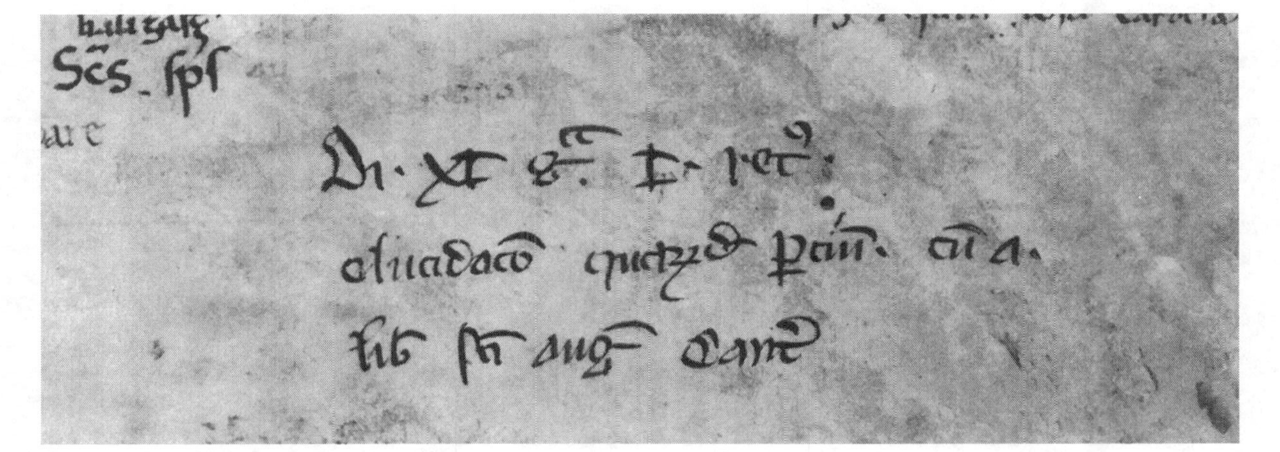

a.

b.

Plate 27 Former ownership marks of Corpus Christi manuscripts from (a) St. Augustine's, Canterbury and (b) Exeter

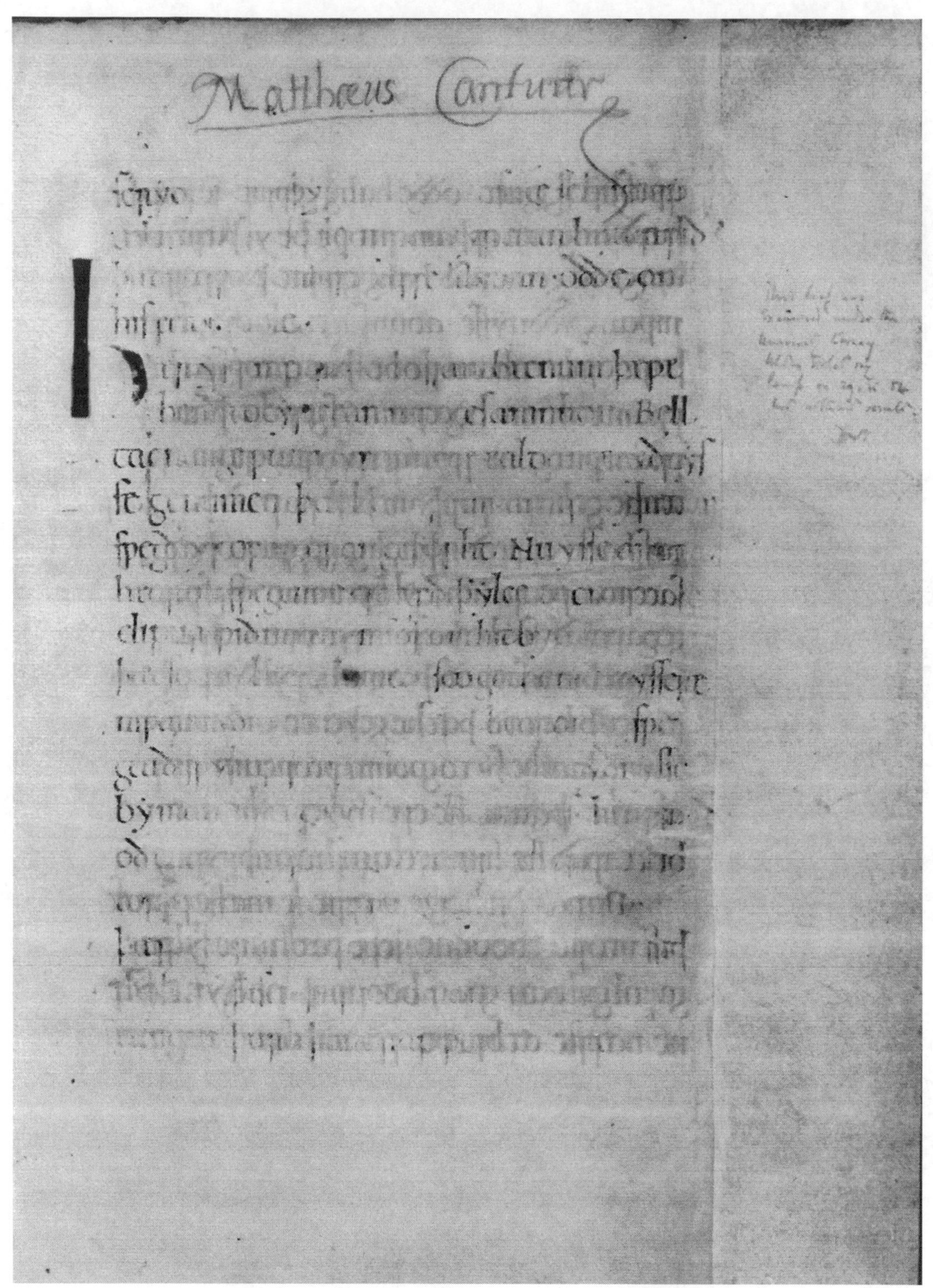

Plate 28 MS CCCC 44, the washed-out p. 1 with Parker's episcopal signature added (reduced)

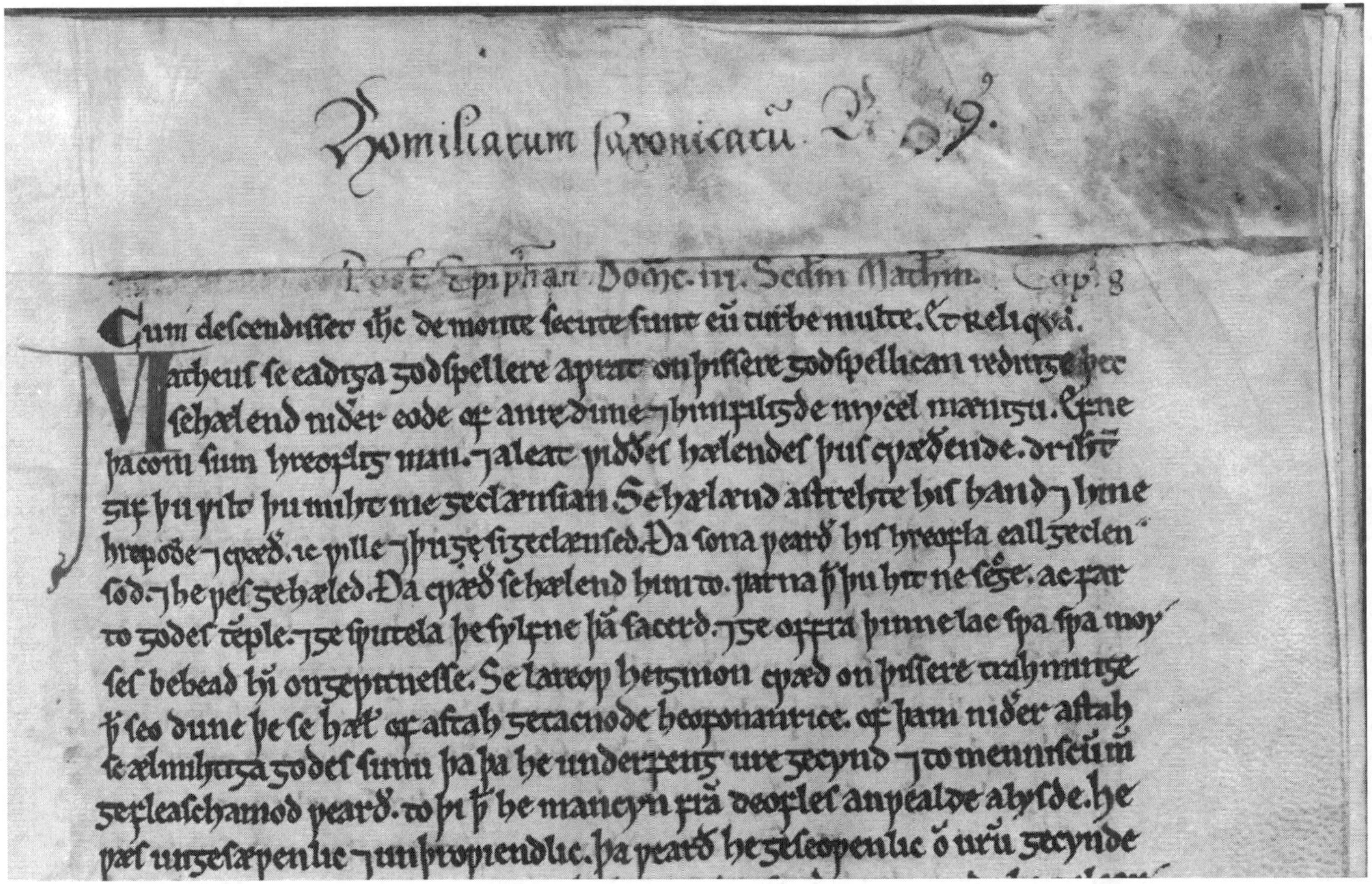

Plate 29 MS CCCC 303 p. 1 with parchment strip covering what remains of the end of a previous item (reduced)

Post epiphan. Dom̄c. iii. Sedm̄ Mathm̄. Cap. 8
Cum descendisset ihc de monte secute sunt eū turbe multe. Et reliquā.
Matheus se eadiga godspellere awrat on þissere godspellican rædinge þet
se hælend nider eode of anre dune 7 him fyligde mycel mangeu. Efne
þa com sum hreoflig man. 7 aleat wiððes hælendes þus cwæðende. drihten
gif þu wilt þu mihte me geclænsian. Se hælend astrehte his hand 7 hine
hrepode 7 cwæð. ic wille 7 þu ge sige clænsed. Ða sona wearð his hreofla eall geclen-
sod. 7 he wes gehæled. Ða cwæð se hælend him to. warna þ þu hit ne segge. ac far
to godes temple. 7 ge swutela þe sylfne þam sacerd. 7 ge offra þinne lac swa swa moy-
ses bebead hi on gewitnesse. Se lareow heimon cwæð on þissere trahtnunge
þ seo dune þe se hæl of astah getacnode heofonan rice. of þam nider astah
se ælmihtiga godes sunu þa þa he underfeng ure gecynd 7 to mennissum
geflæschamod wearð. to þi þ he mancyn fram deofles anwealde alysde. he
wæs ungesewenlic 7 unbegripendlic. þa wearð he gesewenlic on urū gecynde

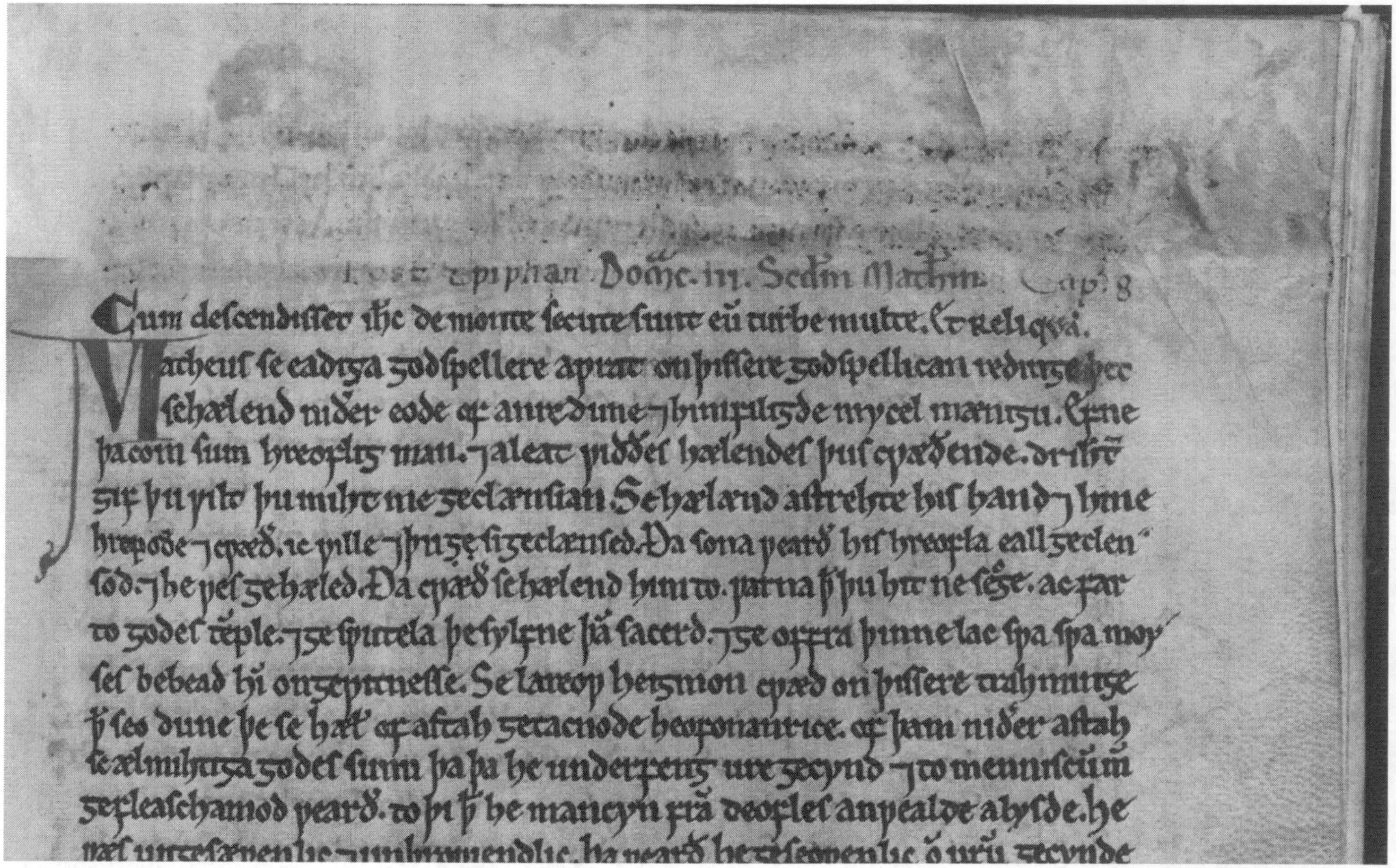

Plate 30 MS CCCC 303 p. 1 with parchment strip removed (reduced)

sig. na be þære declinunge., Gyf ðeo declinatio. þ ys
declinung. sceal toscēadan hwæt gehwylc dæl sig. þon̄ beoð
ealle þas stofon pnomina. þe we nu embe spræcon.
7 eac participia. þ synd dælnymende ge tealde betwux
namum. ac þ ne byð nan gesceād., þas nygon naman
þe we embe sprecað synd apellatiua. þ synd gecigendlice.
ꝑprium nom̄. ys agen nama. 7 apellatiuū byð ælc
oþer nama; Her synd þa naman. quis. hwa. unus. an.
ullus. ænig. nullus. nan. solus. ana. totus. eall. alius.
oþer. oþþe sum. alter. oþer. uter. hwæþer. Ðas naman
synd mobilia: awendenlice. þ tria genera. geond
þreo cynn. Quis. hwa. ys werlic had. Que. hwylc.
ys wiflic. quod. hwylc. nys naþres cynnes. heora ealra
genitiuus byð. Cuius. hwæs. oþþe hwylces. 7 heora ealra
datiuus. Cui. hwam. oþþe hwylcum. quem uirū laudas.
hwylcne wer herast þu. A quo. l a qui. fram hwylcum.
oþþe fram hwā. Et plr. qui. hwylce. oþþe þa. quorū. hwyl[illegible]
oððe þæra. quis l quibus hwylcum. oþþe þam. quos
laudas hwilce herast þu. oððe þa. a quis. l a quibus fram
hwilcū oððe fram þam. Ðes nama hæfð twy fealdne nomi:
natiuū, quis et qui wer hwi bið anfealdes geteles 7 menigfealdes
qui uir se wer. qui uiri þa weras 7 hi habbað. twy fealdne abla:
tiuū, swa swa wecer sædon. Generis feminini, quæ hwylc,
cuius hwylcere. cui. quam. a qua l a qui. et plr. quæ
hwilce. quarū hwilcera. quis. l quibus. quas. a quis. uel a quib:
ac we quib: is gewunelicor. for þan þe quis. is þā oðrum gelic.
Generis neutri. quod hwilc. l quid. oððe þ. cuius hwæs. oððe
hwilces. cui. quod. a quo. l a qui & plr. quæ hwilce oððe þa,
quorū. quis l quib: quæ. a quis. l a quibus. Hit is to
witene þ þas naman habbað. mislic andgit be þan þe hi:
gesette beoð. Gif ic cweðe quis hoc fecit, hwa dyde
þis. þon bið quis. interrogatiuū þ is axigendlic

Plate 31 Sixteenth-century supply text covering the damaged lower half of the defective opening of MS CCCC 449

Plate 32 Sixteenth-century quire added to supply the lost opening of MS CCCC 383, a codex of Anglo-Saxon law texts

Plate 33 MS CCCC 197B fol. 2r, the opening page of St. John's Gospel showing sixteenth-century cropping at the top edge (reduced)

Plate 34 MS CCCC 197B fol. 8r, part of St. John's Gospel showing sixteenth-century cropping of the outer edge of the leaf with damage to the text (reduced)

Plate 35 MS CCCC 557, two binding strips from printed books showing reuse of vellum carrying Old English texts (reduced)

Plate 36 MS CCCC 162 fol. iv^{r}, early sixteenth-century woodcut serving as frontispiece to an Anglo-Saxon manuscript (reduced)

Plate 37 MS CCCC 452, miniature from a thirteenth-century psalter serving as frontispiece to a twelfth-century copy of Eadmer's *Historia novorum*

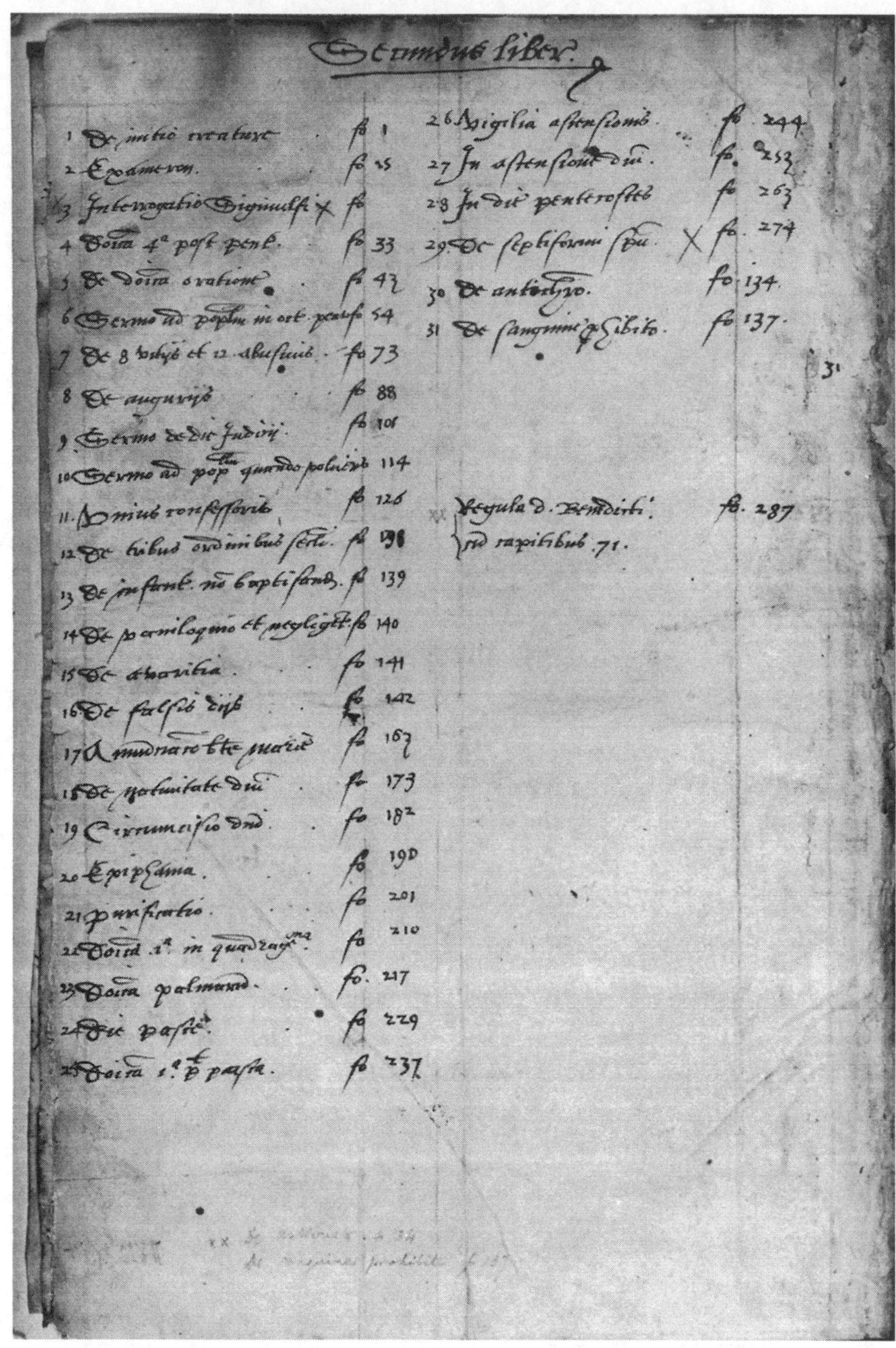

Plate 38 MS CCCC 178 fol. iii^{v}, sixteenth-century contents list of a composite codex comprising an Old English homily book and a Latin-English Rule of St. Benedict (reduced)

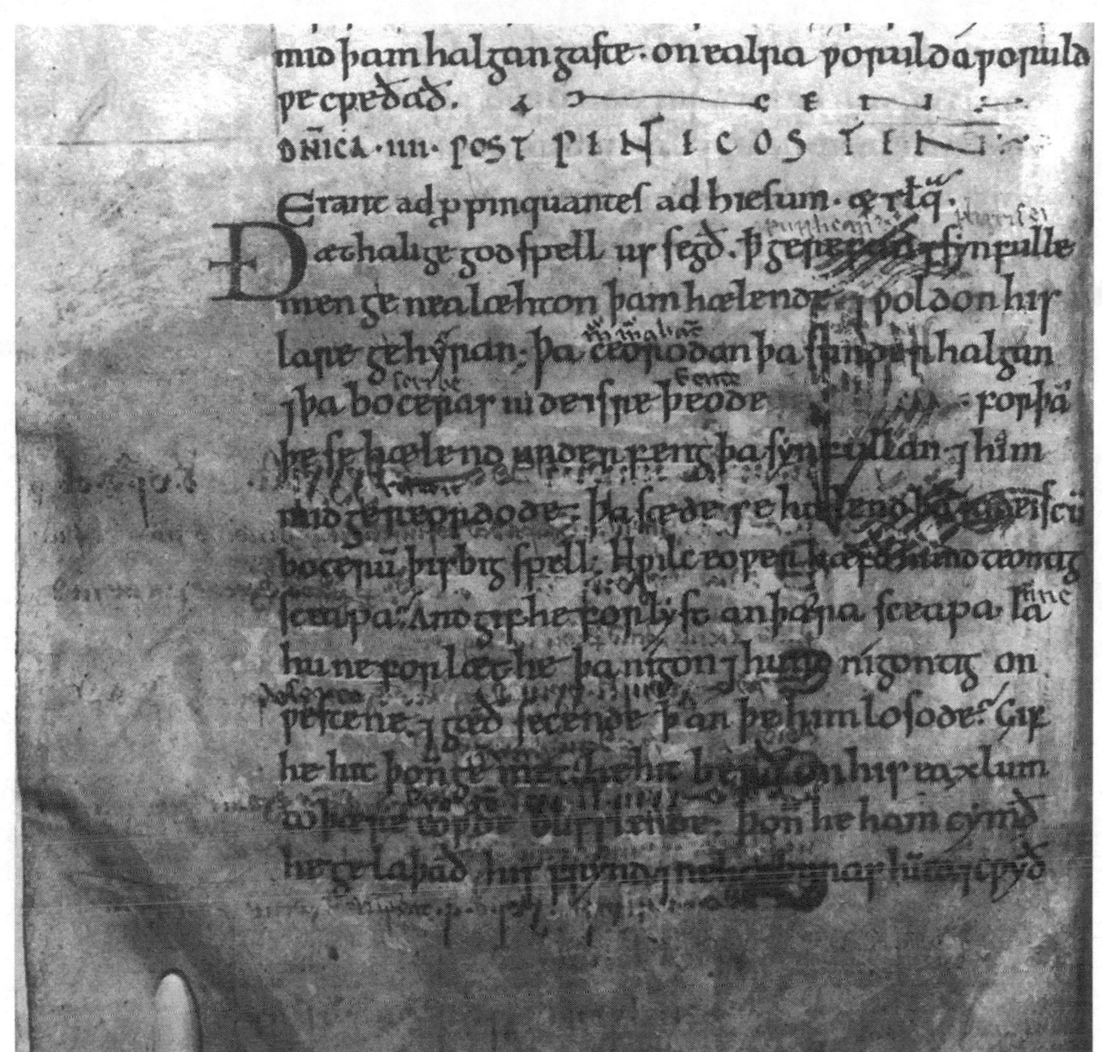

Plate 39 MS CCCC 162 p. 160, opening half-page of a homily removed from MS CCCC 178. The text is much stained by offsetting from the parchment that was used to cover it (reduced)

DOMINICA QVARTA
POST FESTVM PENTECOST.

EVANGELIVM. LVCÆ XV.

Erant autem appropinquantes ei publicani et peccatores ut audirent illum et c.

Plate 40 MS CCCC 178 p. 32, sixteenth-century supply leaf to fill the gap created when this homily opening was removed to MS CCCC 162 (reduced)

Plate 41 CCCC Archives B.3 fol. 89r, eighteenth-century record of the rebinding of MSS CCCC 162 and 178, here given their earlier shelf marks of S.5 and S.6, which were taken to the binders on 26 August 1748 and returned a few days later (reduced)

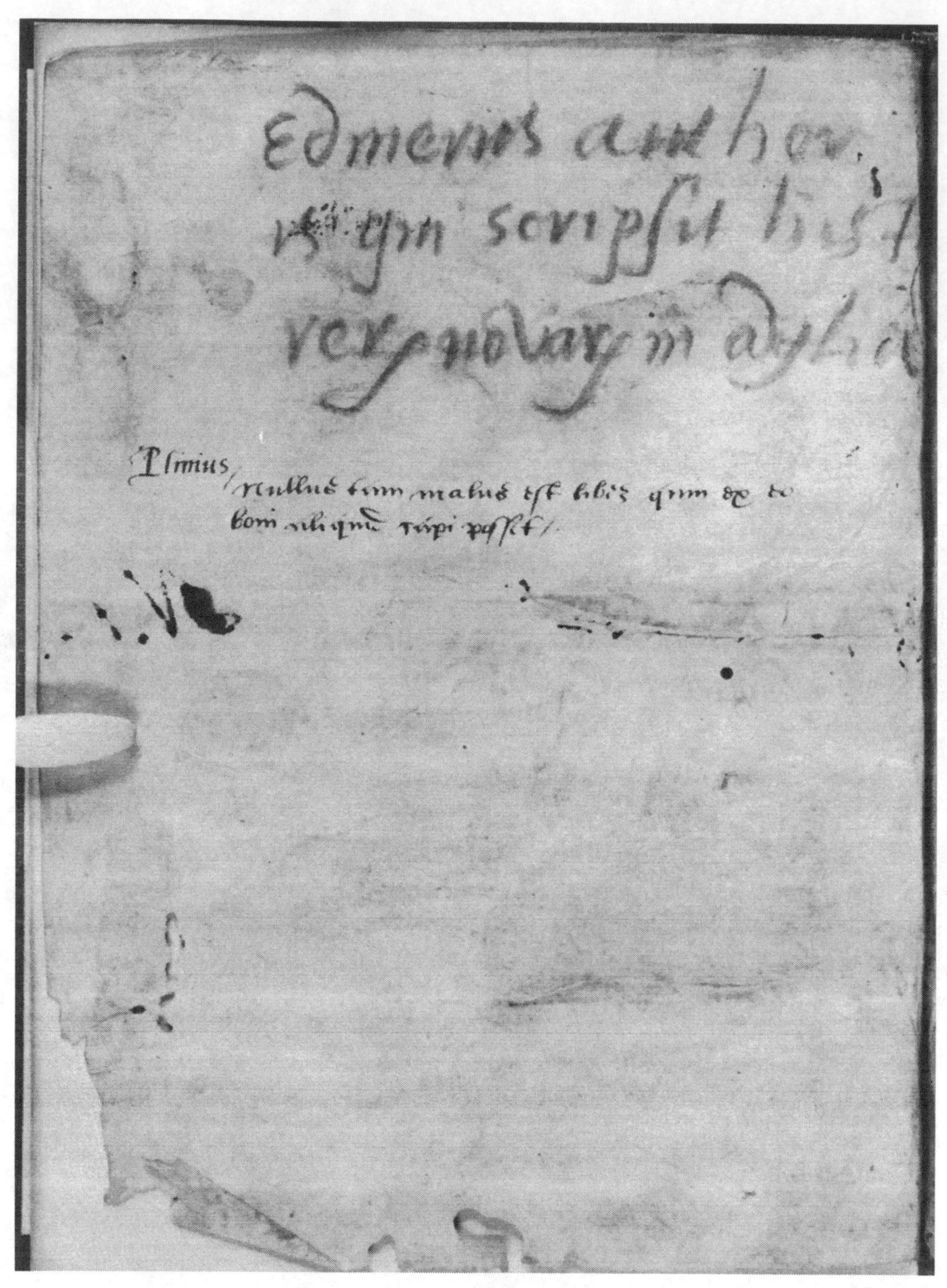

Plate 42 MS CCCC 457, with Parker's note on the historian Eadmer

MATTHAEI PARIS,

in Maiorem historiam Anglorum

post conquisitionem Angliæ, à Duce Normannorum

WILLIELMO,

PROLOGVS.

E CHRONOGRAPHIA, id est, temporum descriptione loquuturi, primò quidem detractatoribus inuidis, & nostrum laborem deputantibus inanem, respōdebimus: deinde beneuolis & id expectantibus, imò depostulantibus, rerum causam præsenti Prologo describemus, ac breuiter aperiemus. Delatores enim dicunt: Quid necesse est vitas vel mortes hominum, diuersosq́ mundi casus literis commendare, prodigia rerum

a.

Præfatio ad Lectorem.

VM nos non nobis solùm natos esse meminerim, (Lector optime) sed Patriæ, Parētibus, & Amicis, istam Thomæ Walsinghami historiam non vni mihi priuatè retinēdam, sed ad communem omnium vtilitatem diuulgandam putaui: idq́ eò

b.

Plate 43 Matthew Parker's arms/initials in his editions of (a) Matthew Paris and (b) Thomas Walsingham (reduced)

OMINO MEO VENERABILI 1.
PIISSIMOQVE OMNIVM BRI
TANNIÆ INSVLÆ CHRISTIA-
NORVM RECTORI ÆLFRED
ANGLORVM SAXONVM RE-
GI: ASSER OMNIVM SERVO-
RVM DEI VLTIMVS MILLE-
MODAM AD VOTA DESIDE-
RIORVM VTRIVSQVE VITÆ PROSPERI-
TATEM.

a.

b.

Plate 44 Matthew Parker's arms/motto in his editions of (a) Asser (reduced) and (b) *Ypodigma Neustriae*

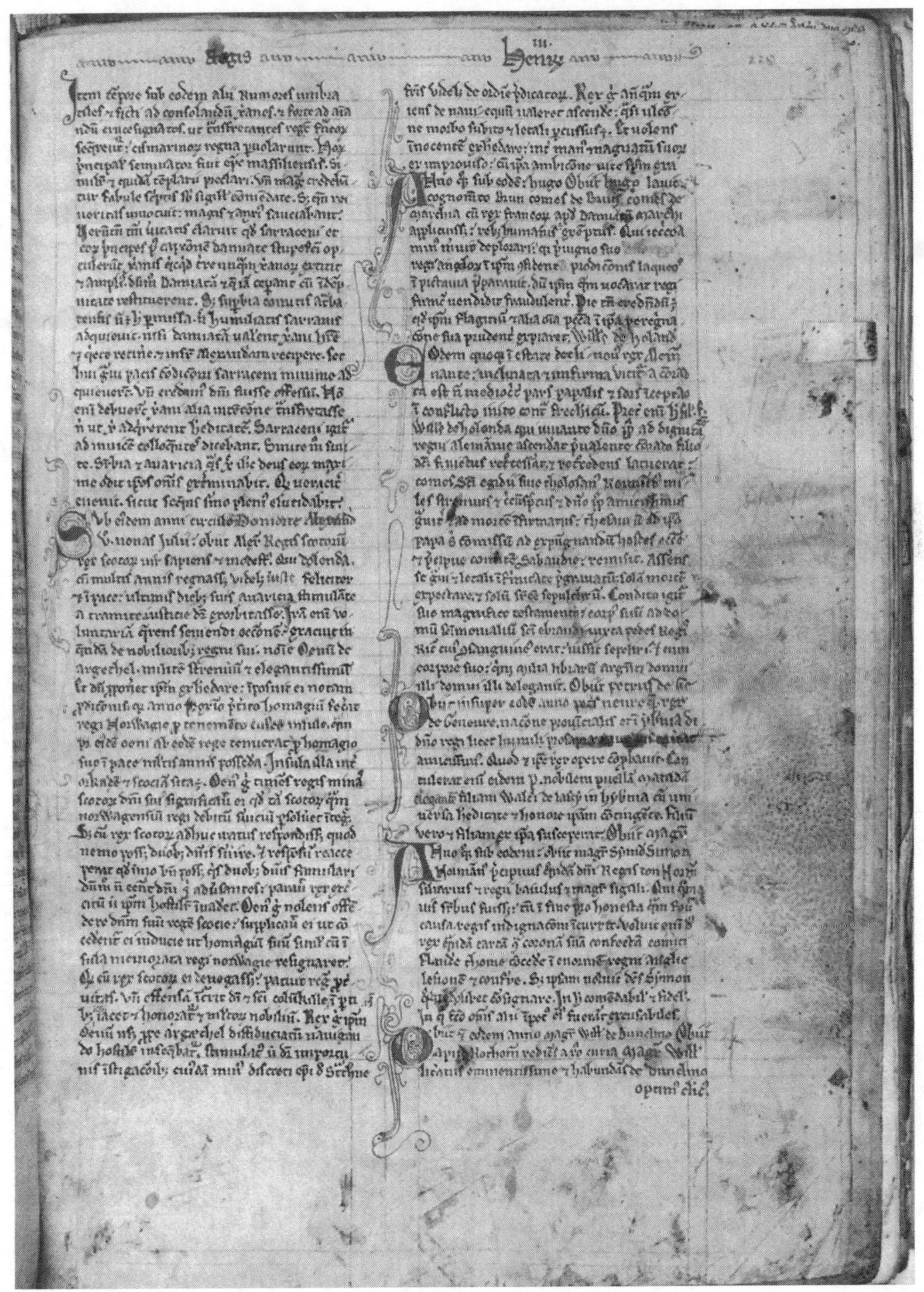

Plate 45 MS CCCC 16 fol. 256r, Matthew Paris's *Historia maiora* used as a copy text, with printer's marginal collations (reduced)

Plate 46 MS CCCC 16 fol. 229r, Matthew Paris's *Historia Maiora* used in the printer's shop (reduced)

Plate 47 MS CCCC 16 fol. 79^{v}, with trace of a wooden block laid across the page to hold it flat in the printer's shop (reduced)

THE CHIEF RETRIEVER OF OUR ANCIENT NATIVE LANGUAGE

Perhaps the most important single book in the field of Anglo-Saxon studies in the twentieth century is N. R. Ker's *Catalogue of manuscripts containing Anglo-Saxon,* published in Oxford in 1957. It is one of those few works of which you can say that you cannot understand how research was done on the subject before it was written. Its range, precision, and perceptivity are extraordinary. I have been amazed, and depressed, to find out how often, as I have laboriously worked through a range of manuscripts to a particular conclusion, Dr. Ker has beaten me to it. Yet occasionally he makes a comment of such ineptitude that one can only take comfort from it. Such a remark occurs in his section on *Ownership and use [of manuscripts], 1540–1603* in the introduction to his volume. Speaking of Matthew Parker he says, "Writing in Parker's hand occurs in very few manuscripts. He was a busy man who left the making of marginalia to others" (Ker 1957:lii). In fact anyone who works through the Parker Library, both printed books and manuscripts, will be amazed at how often his hand occurs, drawing attention to or commenting on the texts. We have Lord Byron's assurance that "We learn from Horace, 'Homer sometimes sleeps'." But to find Dr. Ker not only asleep but snoring loudly is a bit of a surprise.

With these observations I introduce the theme of my last lecture, a consideration of the way Matthew Parker used his manuscripts, and, in particular, those manuscripts which recorded the earliest stages of the English language, for with the Parker collection Corpus Christi keeps one of the three great libraries of Anglo-Saxon manuscripts. As we have seen, John Strype called Parker "the chief Retriever of that our ancient Native Language, the *Saxon* I mean." He added a remark attributed to Parker: "It was worth ones Pains . . . to compare our Country Language, which we now use, with that *obsolete* and almost extinguished Speech; and while we are comparing them, to observe, how like they are, and almost the same" (Strype 1711:535). Strype commented:

> And for that Cause chiefly he took care, that the four Gospels should be printed in that Language, and in the same Form of Character. And that the Reader might the more easily attain the Knowledge and Understanding thereof, the *English* was joined with the *Saxon* in the Margin, and distinguished with such Notes and Signs, that the Sentences of each Language might very readily be compared one with another.

Thus Strype on Parker, educationalist and Anglo-Saxon scholar.

But though Strype gave Parker pre-eminence, he admitted he was not a lone figure. He listed contemporaries such as William Lambarde, student and editor of Anglo-Saxon laws, Laurence Nowell, who, though I think he published no Anglo-Saxon himself, collected and transcribed for others, and John Joscelyn, Parker's amanuensis and a lexicographer by inclination and force of circumstances. Modern scholarship has further enlightened us on the contributions such distinguished amateurs made to the field of Anglo-Saxon scholarship and has added the names of other, and sometimes earlier, students such as Robert Talbot, prebend of Norwich and assiduous annotator of manuscripts, and George Owen, physician and antiquary, who made copies of Old English material. Thus Parker's enthusiasm for the Anglo-Saxon period was not a unique thing: he was following a trend of studies of his time. But by his opportunities, as Archbishop of Canterbury, and by his character, he made himself a leader in this field.

This is the theme of the present lecture, and it is convenient to link it to the group of books I mentioned earlier as published under Parker's patronage and mirroring the ecclesiastical controversies of the age. I begin with the dispute over a married priesthood.

That marriage was an honorable estate even for priests was a contention dear to Parker's heart. He was himself a married priest, and this became a source of friction between himself and his sovereign, who may have had the same beliefs but had different convictions. Nevertheless, article 32 of the Elizabethan Articles of Religion proclaimed that

> Bishops, priests and deacons are not commanded by God's law, either to vow the estate of single life or to abstain from marriage. Therefore it is lawful also for them as for all other Christian men to marry at their own discretion, as they shall judge the same to serve better to godliness.

The subject had been one of dispute for centuries, but the teaching of the Church of England brought it to renewed prominence in England. In defense of his position Parker wrote, or, as is generally said, "inspired," several books. The best-known is *A defence of priestes mariages* published in 1566/67 in reply to Thomas Martin's attack on the institution in 1554 (STC 17518–19). Some say "inspired," yet Parker's hand in this work is both clear and cogent, in particular the use made of his manuscripts—or of manuscripts he had access to—to support the argument. A distinctive example is the way he used MS CCCC 452, the best, perhaps autograph, early text of Eadmer's *Historia novorum*, dating from the twelfth century. This book was certainly one of Parker's favorites. We have seen he decorated its opening with a full-page painting of the meeting of Christ and Mary Magdalene on the morning of the Resurrection. Parker consulted Eadmer's historical work a good deal, for notes in his hand cover the flyleaves, and there is therefore a *prima facie* case for believing that the red crayon underlinings and marginal *nota* signs common in the manuscript are his too. Eadmer's work provided cases to support the Parkerian argument, and many of the later pages of *A defence of priestes mariages* have marginal annotations directing the reader to Eadmer's history. Since in 1567 the *Historia novorum* was available only in manuscript—the *editio princeps* was not until 1623—it is not clear who the marginal references were intended for. Perhaps to overawe adversaries rather than to convince friends. But that they coincide with annotations in CCCC 452 (which are apparently Parker's) is demonstrable.

For instance, when on p. 295 of the printed book the writer cross-references to "Edm. fo. 187," the phrase he quotes, *sponte, nullo pœnitus cogente,* is underlined in red crayon at that point in the manuscript. (Plate 48a and b) Page 308 of the manuscript has the quoted text, *Ego apostolicus sum. & si feceris quod postulo; ab hac te fidei sponsione absoluam.* It has red underlining, and corresponds to the reference, "Edmer," on p. 301 of the printed book. (Plate 49a and b) On p. 305 of *A defence of priestes mariages* is found the marginal reference "Edm.lib 6" alongside an account of the coronation of Henry I's second wife Adela. The manuscript at this point (p. 341) is underlined, this time in black ink, but significantly it has further a marginal cross-reference to other texts added in a hand that is almost certainly Matthew Parker's. (Plates 50a and b) To work through such marginal references in *A defence . . .* is a fascinating occupation, and one that reveals how widely Parker's reading ranged, how well his index system helped him pick up parallels in the most unlikely places. To give an example of such unlikeliness. On p. 328 of *A defence . . .* is the comment, "For euen of late in archbishop Pecchams days they . . . styll prouided agaynst priestes chyldren . . . ," with the marginal "Pecham, anno 1281." (Plate 51a) This reference is not very helpful, and you might look long and hard before finding what it corresponded to. I came upon one answer by chance while leafing through MS CCCC 342, a sixteenth-century copy of that Rochester history which M. R. James identified as a transcript of British Library, Cotton MS Nero D.ii (James 1912:II,175). This transcript shows some few signs of Parkerian intervention, mainly in the matter of underlining personal and place-names. There is little of Parker's marginal notes. Then suddenly, on fol. 110^r, Parker was moved to vigorous reaction by a statement he found in his text. He underlined it and wrote, in a fine bold hand and in his red crayon, the comment "Uxoratus clericus in diebus Johannis Peccham archiepiscopi Cantuariensis." (Plate 51b) And let the Bishop of Rome explain that one away!

A defence . . . has also a number of quotations in Old English (and in the new Anglo-Saxon typeface, about which more anon), some taken from the *Peterborough Chronicle,* that version of the *Anglo-Saxon Chronicle* which was written up in Peterborough in the early twelfth century and which came into the hands of Parker's friend Sir William Cecil. In the facsimile edition of this important manuscript Professor Dorothy Whitelock drew attention to a number of red crayon underlinings and *nota* marks, several of which point to passages quoted by the compiler of *A defence . . .* (Whitelock 1954:22–24). Obviously the *Peterborough Chronicle* was marked up to identify material for use in the book. Whitelock also pointed to a group of annotations in the *Peterborough Chronicle* in an unidentified hand which she traced in certain manuscripts in Parker's collection. She described this hand simply as "sixteenth-century," which it is. What she did not see is that it is also Matthew Parker's. I have already expressed astonishment at finding Dr. Ker fast asleep; it is even more surprising to find Professor Whitelock tucked in beside him.

However, things are seldom as simple as this in Cambridge, and *a fortiori* in Corpus Christi. Let me point out two aspects of Parker's quoting of sources in *A defence . . .* that have to be taken aboard to prevent oversimplifying his contribution to Old English studies. First the way Parker used his sources.

One of his quotations from the *Peterborough Chronicle*, from the entry for 1123, reads (p. 306 in the printed book): "Ða spræcon ða biscopas hem be twenan andsaden þæt hi nefer mare ne wolden hafen munec hades man to ercebiscope ofer hem for þi þæt nefre ne loueden hi munec regol. and se King hit him tidde." The matter is a protest by secular clergy against appointing a celibate, a monk, to be Archbishop of Canterbury. "Then," says the text as Parker quotes it, "the bishops spoke together and said that they never wanted to have a monk as archbishop over them again, because they had never liked the monastic rule. And the king granted them this." Parker's translation, though slightly tendentious at the end, is quite accurate:

> Then spake the byschoppes betweene them selues, and sayd: that they neuer more would haue any man of munkes order to be Archbyshop ouer them, for they neuer alowed nor loued munckes rulyng: and the kyng graunted that to them.

But in his quotation Parker fiddled the evidence. His source gives a more extensive version of the protest. The *Peterborough Chronicle* actually says:

> Then the bishops spoke together and said they never wanted to have a monk as archbishop over them again. They all went together to the king and re-

> quested they might choose whomsoever they wished as archbishop from the ranks of the secular clergy. And the king granted them this. It had all been done through the Bishop of Sarum and the Bishop of Lincoln (before he died), because they never liked the monastic rule but were always against monks and their rule.

Parker or his ghost-writer clearly distorted his source. The effect is to make it appear that it was the whole college of bishops who objected to monasticism. The original shows that the primary objections came from two bishops only. One was the Bishop of Sarum, who was presumably present at the interview with the king. The other, the Bishop of Lincoln, had died some little time before as the *Chronicle* tells. Thus there may have been only one bishop—obviously very persuasive—who dominated the discussion. The objection to celibate rule may have been weaker, less widespread, than Parker's doctored quotation implies. Like all good research students Parker quoted his sources: his external examiner should have had a few words with him about how he used them.

My second point is of a different nature altogether. Among the pieces of Old English quoted in *A defence . . .* is a passage from what is called "Be preosta regul. lxij" (Concerning the priests' rule:62 [p. 346]). The text in question is that now known as the *Enlarged Rule of Chrodegang*. It exists in one manuscript only, CCCC 191. The passage quoted in *A defence . . .* can be easily identified in chapter 62 (p. 127 of the manuscript), where it is the only one heavily annotated. (Plate 52) Above each Old English word is a Latin equivalent. In fact this is an easy bit of the vernacular to translate into Latin because the text of the rule is bilingual. Each chapter is presented first in Latin, then in Old English, and as far as possible the annotator here used the Latin crib to supply his equivalents. But the annotator is certainly not Matthew Parker. Luckily the hand is readily identified. This is the work of John Joscelyn who served for many years as Parker's secretary. Yet Parker himself certainly knew this manuscript, for on p. 164 there is one of his interventions. Next to a passage dealing with clerks in minor holy orders *filios habentes & uxorem*, Parker pondered on the absence of any mention of deacons: "Diaconatus non erat inter sacros ordines." It seems that if we are to keep up the modern analogy, Parker was not a research student. Rather a director of research, with a research associate (Joscelyn) and presumably several research assistants.

It is the impression of a vigorous, tenacious, organized, and enquiring mind that one gets in observing Matthew Parker's relationship to his books. It is not that he had a specially wide range of interests, at any rate as far as I have traced them in my work. Indeed, he searched his books for a comparatively limited type of material, specifically engaging a few major professional topics: the history and nature of the Church of England, the relationship between church and state and between the English church and the Bishop of Rome, the primacy of the see of Canterbury; certain major themes of church discipline or practice, as the marriage of priests or the translation of the scriptures into a tongue understanded of the people; certain aspects of doctrinal controversy, as the nature of the eucharist. However, I am more inclined than I was when I began this work to give to Parker much of the credit for what was done on his books, rather than attributing it to fellow-workers and assistants as some scholars seem happy to do.

A further example, to which I drew attention in 1983, involves a virtually unknown book with the title *Prosper his meditation with his wife*. The sole surviving copy is bound with the manuscript material of CCCC 448. The date of printing is unknown, perhaps (if STC 20444.5 is correct) c.1570. The printer was the little-known Richard Watkins. Whether this book was ever published or not we do not know—the CCCC 448 copy may be a proof only—but it is certainly included in the list of books for which Parker gained credit in Lambeth Palace MS 959, where it is defined as *Epigrammata varia Prosperj cum coniuge in rithmo Anglico*. The contents comprise a group of verses allegedly written by Prosper of Aquitaine to his wife, and since Prosper, at least in Parker's belief, was a bishop of the Catholic church, this showed that in the fifth century the church had married bishops. *A defence* . . . had already drawn attention to this point (p. 271), and if in fact the Prosper book was printed c.1570, it can be seen as adding further documentation to the argument. Thus the Watkins book was linked to the circle engaged in controversy over priests' marriages, and annotations in some of Parker's own books attach it firmly to the archbishop himself (Page 1983a).

The Prosper text used as a base for the 1570 edition was itself a printed one, that of the 1539 Lyon edition that Parker later bequeathed to the College (B.4.16). In 1983 I demonstrated that a group of manuscript annotations to this volume were the source of items in the introduction to the Watkins printed text. (Plate 53) I have to admit I described these annotations as in one or more "sixteenth-century hands." Now it is clear to me that at least two of them are in Matthew Parker's: if Dr. Ker and Professor Whitelock were sleeping, I was bundling in with them too. It may be that all five notes are in Parker's hand at various stages of writing, development, carefulness of script; that I am less sure of. But that these annotations of Parker's are represented in Watkins's introduction is certain. There also seems to be a connection with the citation from Prosper in Parker's CCCC MS 14 text of Vincent of Beauvais's *Speculum historiale*. One further point. Watkins gave Prosper's verses a facing translation into banal and limping English verse. There are a couple of manuscript corrections to the text of this translation, and they too look to be in Parker's hand. (Plate 54) The English verses have the same indifferent quality as does Parker's translation of the psalter, which he published in (?) 1567 (STC 2729). I suspect the Prosper translation is another example of the proud full sail of Parker's great verse.

Indeed, the edition makes sense only if we assume that Parker was the translator. Though the title-page is in English, its note on the author (*A*2a) and the note to the reader (E3b) are both in Latin, which therefore the reader is assumed to command. To serve its purpose no translation of Prosper's verses into English was necessary. The translation must have had some other intent, and the gratification of poetic vanity may be it.

Parker's defense of married priests also appears, though tangentially, in another work published at the archbishop's instigation at about the same time as these others. This work is *A testimonie of antiquitie* whose two states STC 159 and 159.5, are tentatively dated (?) 1566. In a classic article John Bromwich defined this as "the first book printed in Anglo-Saxon types" (Bromwich 1962). His evidence for the precedence of at any rate the two preliminary printings of this work to other books using the typeface is in part the state of the font: it gives "a very sharp impression" and has "suffered little wear and tear." Thus it is, he thinks, the first attempt to print Old English in a special typeface approximating to Anglo-Saxon manuscript forms which, by tradition, Parker had made and used by his favorite printers, John Day and Henry Bynneman. (It is interesting to note that typefaces of this sort continued in use for Old English into the nineteenth century and that Dr. Leslie French has reintroduced this form of presentation using graphs created by computer methods).

In *A testimonie of antiquitie* the question of priests remaining celibate is of secondary importance. It is mentioned only in the preface as one of those fond things vainly invented in the more recent history of the Roman church. The main thrust of *A testimonie of antiquitie* is doctrinal, interested in showing that Parker's Church of England was in essential matters more closely allied to the early Christian church in this country than was his contemporary Roman church. The preface begins, "Great contention hath nowe been of longe tyme about the most comfortable sacrament of the body and bloud of Christ our Sauiour," and that is the theme of the book—Parker's determination to show that the Anglo-Saxon church, as his own reformed church, did not believe in the doctrine of transubstantiation which, as article 28 of the Articles of Religion proclaimed, was "repugnant to the plain words of Scripture . . . and hath given occasion to many superstitions."

The substance of *A testimonie . . .* is a text and translation of an Easter sermon written by Ælfric, the late tenth-/early eleventh-century West Saxon homilist. Though Parker admitted that even Ælfric's church was "full of blindnes and ignoraunce" and "ouermuch cumbred with monckery," yet Ælfric was, he asserted, sound on the eucharist. The body and blood of the church service is "naturally corruptible bread, & corruptible wine: and is by mighte of Godes worde truely Christ's bodye, and his bloude: not so notwithstanding bodely, but ghostly," or as Ælfric put it himself, *na swaþeah lichamlice. ac gastlice* (fols. 34^{v}–35^{r}).

Ker's *Catalogue* lists five manuscripts containing this Ælfrician homily. Of these Bromwich noted two which were particularly closely linked to the printing of *A testimonie . . .*: British Library, Cotton Faustina A ix and CCCC 198. Both manuscripts have sixteenth-century annotations, cross-referencing the manuscript text to that of the printed book. *A testimonie . . .* has two issued states: (i) with the preface unfoliated and the homily numbered 1–42; (ii) with the preface foliated, so that the homily should be 19–60, but in fact there are blunders in the typesetting and the final folio is numbered 61. In the two manuscripts under examination the sixteenth-century annotator (who was probably not

Parker) marked off the equivalents of the printed pages by ink slashes and underlinings and added in the margin both possible printed paginations: these two paginations were entered at different times but apparently by the same writer. (Plate 55) It is not that he was marking up the copy for the printing press for there is no evidence that either manuscript visited the printer's shop: no sign of heavy handling or of printer's ink. Someone was presumably marking up the manuscripts so that the printed texts could be checked off from them. Bromwich suggests that the manuscripts were thus annotated "by someone skilled in the [Anglo-Saxon] language, so that they could be compared with the printed folios by a person or persons, who were not printers, and who may not have been skilled in Anglo-Saxon" (Bromwich 1962:279); specifically, that the marks were to guide the group of bishops of the Church of England who confirmed the accuracy of the text for controversial purposes. On the whole Bromwich made his case, though there remains the problem of the innumeracy of the printer of the second state of *A testimonie. . . .* His blundering of the homily's folio numbering is not reproduced in the annotation of these manuscripts so there are discrepancies in cross-referencing the later pages: which would cause checking difficulties.

So far Bromwich. There follows on him Dr. T. H. Leinbaugh who studied the publication of this sermon in the context of sixteenth-century Anglican polemics. Leinbaugh pointed out, correctly, that certain parts of Ælfric's sermon as it is preserved in MSS Cotton Faustina A ix, CCCC 198, and elsewhere do not fit comfortably with the Anglican view of the nature of the eucharist (Leinbaugh 1982:54–55). Notably, two miracle stories that appear in the middle of Ælfric's homily seem to show something more solid in the celebration of the Lord's supper than its "heavenly and spiritual manner." The first of the miracles suggests a strong physical presence of the body of Christ in the host. It tells of two monks who needed assurance on the point. As they attended mass they saw laid out on the altar a child, and above it an angel with drawn sword. As the celebrant broke the bread, the angel sliced up the child and its blood flowed into the chalice. When they came to take the eucharist, the child's body had turned to bread, the blood to wine. A second, not dissimilar, story follows. These tales were embarrassing to the editors of *A testimonie . . .* , and they put in the margin of their text the note, "These tales seme to be infarced," to which the second state adds "placed here vpon no occasion" (fol. 39r). Summing up the discussion later on in the book (fol. 76) Parker—or his assistants—appeal to literary criticism, claiming that the miracle stories "stand in their place vnaptly, and without purpose, and the matter without them, both before & after, doth hange in it selfe together most orderly," with which I would agree. To Leinbaugh this dismissal of the miracle tales was a "cavalier attitude toward the integrity of Ælfric's text"—if the homily contained something that did not fit the Anglican position, the editors of *A testimonie* . . . rejected it as an interpolation. In fact, however, Parker was anything but cavalier about the text, as a closer examination of the archbishop's interventions in his manuscripts would have revealed (Page 1983b:444–45). For instance, in MS CCCC 162 there is a text of a quite different Easter homily, which inevitably turns on Christ's self-sacrifice and its link with the eucharist (pp. 382–91). This homily includes passages which coincide almost exactly with passages in the homily of *A testimonie* . . . (pp. 387–89). They include the two miracle stories. Parker spotted this and concluded, presumably correctly, that these tales must be interpolations into either the homily of CCCC 162 or that of *A testimonie* . . . (or of course both). Since he felt that the structure of *A testimonie* . . . did not require the miracle stories, he may have concluded, on adequate grounds, that they had been "infarced" into that text. That Parker noticed the relationship between the homilies of CCCC 162 and *A testimonie* . . . is shown by his annotations on pp. 387–89 of CCCC 162. In the margin of p. 387 he wrote, in red crayon, "In Libello Impresso" and also gave a reference to the pagination of the first issue of *A testimonie*. . . . (Plate 56) He then marked off the beginning and end of each passage of common material. Finally, he tagged the foot of the page to make it easy to refer to. This could be further assistance to the bishops checking the acceptability of the argument presented in *A testimonie*. . . .

Parker—or his men—also collated two other texts of this homily, those in MSS CCCC 302 and Cambridge University Library, Ii.4.6, a manuscript Parker gave to the University Library in 1574. In these cases there are no written annotations, only red pencil marks that indicate where significant common omissions begin and end: we cannot be sure this is Parker, but it is most likely. From this brief survey of the evidence it is clear that whatever Parker was, he was not cavalier about the text. Indeed, if there is anyone being cavalier, it is Dr. Leinbaugh rather than Dr. Parker.

There is a further point to be made about these annotations to MS CCCC 162. They allow us to give some date to Parker's interventions. The reference to the printed book shows that the comment could not have been made before 1566, and the fact that the reference is to the first (and I think relatively rare) state of the book suggests it was not much later than that date. Thus this work was done at the heart of Parker's occupancy of the see of Canterbury. His devoted work towards consolidating the administration of the Elizabethan church settlement did not prevent him from spending a lot of time in manuscript study.

To understand and quote these sources—and even more to misquote or adapt them meaningfully—Parker and his men needed some knowledge of Old English, not a particularly easy thing to come by in the mid sixteenth century. I say "Parker and his men" though some recent scholars have denied that Parker himself had any such knowledge, preferring to believe that most of the work requiring any acquaintance with early English was done by others, and in particular by Joscelyn. I do not underestimate the important contribution that Joscelyn made—his own transcripts and translations of Old English and his contribution to an Old English dictionary are evidence here—but I have no doubt that Parker also knew something of the tongue. His hand annotating the Peterborough and Parker *Chronicles* (and even Dr. Ker accepts the latter) as well as a number of other vernacular works is a clear sign of his awareness of the nature of Old English, to some extent at least. I am not sure how accurately. Whether he would have got more than an upper second in the Anglo-Saxon, Norse, and Celtic Tripos I do not know, though since he commonly wrote his name at the head of the page, he would have got at least 20%. In my second lecture I identified Parker himself as the scribe who wrote out a passage of Old English to fill the lacuna he had created in MS CCCC 178. (Plate 57) His copying had errors, and errors that showed him weak in aspects of formal grammar as well as vocabulary. He miscounted minims, and produced, instead of the correct dative plural *-um*, the impossible *-wn*. He confused *s* and *f*. He read *þis* as *his*, interpreting the distinctive Anglo-Saxon letter *thorn* as *h*. He misdivided one word. Less seriously he modernized spellings, adding an inorganic *-e* to the ends of words (as he would have done with his own English) or replacing *y* by *i* (Page 1973:80–81).

In these respects he resembled other sixteenth-century scholars and clerics who achieved quite a respectable understanding of the language. The translation of *A testimonie* . . . has a similar collection of elementary errors: in morphology with singulars for plurals and present tenses for past, and so on. Yet here the general sense, and often a good deal more than the general sense, is rendered. Parker was obviously the guiding figure in these related projects, and to this extent must indeed be thought of as "the chief Retriever of that our ancient Native Language."

This should make us curious to know how Parker and his helpers learned to manipulate this dead language, with its comparatively complex noun, adjective, and verb systems, and its not easily recognizable vocabulary. They had predecessors, so they were not beginning from scratch, but they had neither grammars nor detailed dictionaries. How then did they achieve their command?

(1) A knowledge of the Old English lexis they gained in part from studying Latin-Old English glossaries, such as the Anglo-Saxons themselves compiled. The sixteenth century used these in the opposite sense to the Anglo-Saxons, approaching the unknown Old English through the known Latin, rather than the other way round. Chief among these glossaries was the *Corpus Glossary*, MS CCCC 144, a ninth-century manuscript of uncertain provenance but which was for a time at St. Augustine's, Canterbury. (Plate 58a) This is an alphabetical glossary in AB order. It has both Latin-Latin glosses (for those who already knew some Latin words and wanted access to more learned ones) and Latin-Old English glosses (simple cribs). In the manuscript the latter have been underlined, and since Joscelyn (in collaboration later with John Parker) compiled Old English word lists with modern English translations, it is possible this underlining was connected with that project. But MS CCCC 144 is a glossary in impressive format. Parker's men could use less imposing word-lists too. One such is part of MS CCCC 183, Bede's verse and prose lives of St. Cuthbert. Between the two lives is set a list of fifty-one Latin words taken from the verse life, with equivalents, either Latin or Old English. In nearly every case the Old English form has been picked out by a dot placed before the word. (Plate 58b) Since

Parker is known to have been active with this manuscript (for he, I think, added names to the list of Archbishops of Canterbury), it is not unlikely that he picked out these words for collection. But alas it is hard to establish a typology of dots which will allow us to identify his hand with certainty. One other group of manuscripts contributed to the understanding of Old English lexis: those of the grammar and glossary of the Anglo-Saxon scholar Ælfric. Parker recognized the importance of these texts, and three manuscripts of them passed through his hands. Only one remains in the Parker Library, CCCC 449. The opening of the glossary (fol. 89^{r}) has a Parkerian note appended to the page: "littere significant numerum in dictionario novo." (Plate 59) The outer margins of the text hold a sequence of letters and thereafter numbers, drawing attention to Latin words with their Old English equivalents, underlined for lexical purposes.

(2) At the same time, Ælfric's grammar too could be used by readers wanting to learn something of the shape of the Old English language. Ælfric designed his Latin grammar for the instruction of Anglo-Saxon students, but it could be used in reverse by sixteenth-century enquirers wishing to learn Old English.

(3) Particularly useful to such scholars were those Old English works for which a contemporary Latin crib was available. Some Old English texts were translations of important Latin originals, and it could happen that a manuscript had both Latin and Old English versions in close proximity. We saw one example of this in the *Enlarged Rule of Chrodegang.* Another case is in MS CCCC 178 whose second part is the Rule of St. Benedict in the two languages, chapter by chapter. On p. 291, at the bottom of the facing opening chapters of the two versions, Parker wrote in his characteristic red crayon: "In hoc Libro facilius discitur Lingua saxonica." (Plate 60)

(4) The same manuscript indicates another method whereby Old English could be learned. Its texts had already been glossed in the thirteenth century by the "tremulous Worcester hand"; so there was available to the sixteenth-century reader a set of glosses over the Old English words. The "tremulous Worcester" scribe was a man of great application, and numbers of manuscripts with his annotations survive. In the thirteenth century he took upon himself an interest in the—by now dead—Old English tongue. Over some, and perhaps many, years he

taught himself the old language, in part by comparing Old English translations with their Latin originals rather as, though perhaps more adventurously than, the Parkerian group of Anglo-Saxonists did. He glossed his Old English texts, sometimes in Latin, sometimes in his contemporary version of Middle English, and it is clear that Parker and his men took note of the glosses thus presented to them. In one case it is possible to demonstrate unambiguously the influence of the Worcester hand on the Parkerian circle. This involves a passage in the Easter homily text of *A testimonie* . . . (STC 159.5 fols. 30^{v}–31^{r}). The homilist tries to explain how Christ was frequently likened, symbolically, to a variety of other things. The original text says, "he is gecweden hlaf ðurh getacnunge. and lamb. & leo. and gehu elles." The translation is, "He is sayd bread by signification, & a lambe, & a lyon, & a mountayne." Now this contains an absurdity. The translation is sensible up to the last word, then it goes crazy: what the Old English says is that Christ is called "bread" by token, and "lamb," and "lion," and various other things (*gehu elles*). How then did the "mountayne" get into the argument? What made Parker and his men think that the phrase *gehu elles* could mean "mountain"? The answer is in MS CCCC 198, fol. 220^{r}, which was annotated by the "tremulous Worcester hand." From somewhere, I do not know where or why, that scribe got the parallel *mons* and wrote it over the first part of the divided phrase *gehu / elles.* (Plate 61) Parker took over this erroneous gloss and anglicized it as "mountayne."

Today, perhaps the best-known piece of Old English prose is King Alfred's prefatory letter to the ninth-century translation of Gregory the Great's *Cura pastoralis*. This preface takes the form of a circular letter sent to the bishops of Alfred's land. It is a fine piece of writing studied by all beginners in Old English and with good reason. It defines the sad state of literacy and learning in the England of the later ninth century and outlines Alfred's plans for a revival, showing a mind of distinction applying itself energetically to a practical problem. Briefly Alfred describes the great age of English civilization, when foreigners came to this country because of the high quality of its system of further education, and compares it with his own day when Englishmen must go abroad to get learning. The decline in literacy Alfred attributes in part to the Vikings, as nowadays we blame Shirley Williams. Even the clergy needed teaching, and for this Alfred relied, as perhaps we cannot, on a learned bench of bishops.

It is easy to see why such a passage should attract Parker's attention. In 1560/61 he had been busy compiling a directory of clergy for the dioceses of his province. For each incumbent he had asked for details—whether married or not, whether he preached, whether he resided in his benefice, and so on. One of the questions asked for information on the curate's learning. Was he *doctus*? The returns of Parker's diocesans survive, as MSS CCCC 97, 122, and 580. They make gloomy reading. Some clergy were *docti*; others *mediocriter docti*; others again *indocti* or even *omnino indocti*; and some specifically *Latine indocti*. Parker could sympathize with Alfred.

There was a further topical theme in the prefatory letter, the translation of books from Latin and other languages into contemporary English. Alfred pondered what he could do to ensure that there was a wider spread of learning in his country. He came up with the plan of compulsory education for all young men (perhaps even young people) who had the appropriate rank—free and of independent means—to be set to learning as long as they were not ready for any other duty in society. They were to be taught to read English. Those picked for higher office could be taught further and learn Latin. One of the needs was text books, so Alfred set out a plan of translating "those books that are most needful for all men to know" into English. One of his first choices was Gregory's book on pastoral care. In so doing, argued Alfred, he was following the practice of centuries, for each language community had made a habit of translation, particularly of the Bible and its law; from Hebrew to Greek, then to Latin, then to the vernaculars. Obviously a statement like this was just up Matthew Parker's street, and he and his colleagues used the Alfredian material for their own ends. Caius quoted from it in his book on the antiquity of the University of Cambridge (Caius 1568:286–87). Foxe mentioned it to justify the publication of the Old English version of the Gospels with parallel contemporary English translation (Foxe 1571:Aiiij). And there is a full text and literal interlinear translation, together with a rendering into Latin, as an appendix to some issues of the Asser *Life of Alfred*.

Alfred's letter to his bishops survived into modern times in five manuscripts. Two of them were in the Cotton Library, Otho B.ii and

Tiberius B.xi. Both suffered in the conflagration of 1731, and the second was almost completely destroyed in a second fire in 1865. The texts of their prefaces are known now virtually only from seventeenth-century transcripts. Both manuscripts were apparently complete in Parker's time, and Joscelyn certainly knew Otho B.ii (Ker 1957:lii).

Today's three surviving texts of the preface are Cambridge University Library MS Ii.2.4, given by Parker in 1574, and CCCC 12, also Parkerian; and Bodleian Library MS Hatton 20, apparently sent by Alfred to Worcester and still there in Parker's day. Hatton 20 is lightly glossed in the tremulous hand. CCCC 12, also from Worcester, is highly glossed in that hand, and Joscelyn copied into Hatton 20 some of the CCCC 12 glosses, so he had the opportunity to compare both texts. CUL Ii.2.4 was given an interlinear translation into English perhaps by Joscelyn, and it is this that is the basis of the text and translation published in 1574. (Plate 62) There are two further translations to be taken into account. In his commonplace book of early materials, the *Collectanea* (MS Cotton Vitellius D.vii) Joscelyn copied the text and wrote a translation of the *Cura pastoralis* letter taken from Hatton 20. Attached to the opening of CCCC 197A (but first recorded there only in the eighteenth century) is a translation in an unknown sixteenth-century hand with a heading in Parker's. (Plate 63) So the work had a lot of activity on it in Parkerian times, and it is interesting to see what this reveals.

One thing to note is that in many ways the thirteenth-century glossator had a better command of Old English than did the sixteenth century. He was better at verbal tenses and noun numbers. He could distinguish homographs. He knew that *þa* may sometimes be the conjunction "then," sometimes the plural article; and he took care to note this. He knew that *hie* was a pronoun, but its form could be the nominative plural "they" or the feminine accusative singular "her." And so on. The sixteenth-century scholars are sometimes confused in such cases. The "tremulous Worcester hand" gets word meanings right when the sixteenth century, though having a correct gloss to guide it, gets them wrong. One example is Alfred's claim that in earlier days English kings flourished *ge mid wige ge mid wisdome* (both with warfare and with wisdom). The Asser text (as Ii.2.4) translates this "aswell in witte asin wisdome." But *mid wige* cannot mean "in wit." Even the tremulous glossator got this wrong at first. In MS CCCC 12 he rendered the word as though it were *sige* (which it somewhat resembles), putting *victoria*. Later, or at least when he was more tremulous, he amended this to *bello* (MS CCCC 12), *proelio* (MS Hatton 20), which is correct. MS CCCC 197A gets it right, "warre." "Witte" is sheer idleness on someone's part.

The different sixteenth-century treatments of this piece require a study in themselves. Suffice it to say here that translations are often more by guess than by skill: for instance, when in the opening sentence Alfred greets the recipient bishop *his wordum* (in his own words), the phrase is taken to mean "his worthy bishop" in defiance of grammar and word order. Some words baffled both the tremulous scribe and the sixteenth-century commentators. When Alfred describes how former kings kept *ge heora sybbe ge heora sydo*, the last word was a difficulty. It means something like "morality, code of behavior." The tremulous glossator put *collaterales* here, linking it with OE *side* (side). The Asser text has "expedition of war" (as Ii.2.4), apparently a confusion with OE *siþ* (journey, expedition). In the *Collectanea* and MS CCCC 197A the word seems to be rendered "coastes," again I suppose a connection with "side." In this case the translators are all floundering, trying to find a word that will fit the context, "both their peace and their *sydo*.

I am aware that in speaking in this series about Parker's work I have approached more subjects than I have explored. Here is a vast field of research. We clearly need a critical edition of the Parker Register. But we must also:

(1) Learn to distinguish between the different hands that annotate Parker's books and date them. Can we be sure of Parker's italic and secretary hands, of the various writers who supplied transcripts of earlier work, of his immediate staff and his helpers, of those who imitate earlier scripts?

(2) Examine in detail the miscellaneous manuscripts of the collection. Can we compare their definitions in the Parker Register with their present states, and from this can useful conclusions be drawn? Does it help to examine make-up, the various early paginations, the watermarks of the different batches of paper; from that can we determine anything of the way they came to be as they are? Can conclusions drawn from miscellaneous manuscripts be applied to other composite codices in the collection?

(3) Find out if the Parkerian contents lists in the manuscripts tell us

anything. Do they agree with the present contents or not? What do the page-numberings supplied to them tell us? Are the contents lists added to or subtracted from?

(4) Try to establish the purposes Parker had in assembling his collection. Why did he annotate? How extensively did he study the various sorts of books he acquired? To what extent did he use books borrowed from other owners?

(5) Check differences between books he left in Corpus Christi College's keeping and those that ultimately went to other institutions—in binding, in annotation, in intervention, in content. Can we be sure that all so-called Parker books were really part of Parker's own library?

Clearly I have asked here more questions than I have answered. But I take refuge in Ibsen's retort in a verse letter to his young friend Georg Brandes:

> Kræv ikke, ven, at jeg skal gåden klare;
> Jeg spørger helst; mit kald er ej at svare.
>
> (My friend, don't ask me to solve the problem.
> I prefer asking questions. Answering them is not my job.)

Looking back over a quarter of a century in charge of Matthew Parker's books, I look back with gratitude on the collaboration I have enjoyed with colleagues from many lands. I also remember with pleasure scholars and friends who have helped me understand and appreciate the immense treasures that Corpus Christi College has under its care and which—in some small way—it still applies its resources and skills to keep. I cannot list them all, but I must at least hold in memory here one Parker Librarian, Dr. Patrick Bury, most generous and courteous of scholars, and two professorial colleagues, Bruce Dickins and Christopher Cheney, who with their various and brilliant talents taught me much and—what is perhaps more important—untaught me so much more.

Within the present frame of the library I must also express my thanks to younger colleagues whose assistance in preparing these lectures has been immense. Mildred Budny has shared some of her far-reaching experience of early English and Continental manuscripts, and her skills in photography have enlivened what would otherwise have been something of a dry and formal study. Tim Graham, coming fresh to the examination of our collection, has by his questioning made us often look anew at familiar things and learn to collect different forms of evidence. And from a slightly different field, Catherine Hall, with her specialist training in archive work, has helped me establish, or sometimes question, the nature of the material I use.

In the end, however, it is to Matthew Parker that I look back, and my present studies have served only to increase my respect for this great man. He stands as a monument of industry and integrity. He is not one of the glamorous figures of our sixteenth-century history, but I sense in him an honesty and firmness of purpose which may have been as rare in his own time as it is in ours. He addressed himself to the many problems his newly established church encountered, and, in the face of envy, hatred, and malice, and all uncharitableness, he met with courage those whose genius lay in finding fault and speaking slander. Only occasionally did his stoicism break down and allow him to speak the truth in love of "a bragging brainless head or two" (Bruce and Perowne 1853:246), when he felt betrayed and traduced by those he might have expected to support and help him. Like later keepers of the Parker Library he soon learned to "bear to hear the truths he'd spoken / Twisted by knaves to make a trap for fools." He bore this new learning with dignity.

But this is too wry a quotation to end a series of lectures on Parker with. He was not unwelcoming to the good things of this world as his correspondence shows. He thought the office of Primate of All England should bring with it a proper archiepiscopal demeanor and entertainment. Therefore I end on a cheerful and worldly note. In the Old English translation of the Gospels that he gave to the University Library (Ii.2.11) Parker occasionally annotated points that interested him. When he came to Luke 1.xv, a description of the prophecies of the birth of John the Baptist, he found the phrase, "and he shall drink neither wine nor strong drink" (*he ne drincþ win ne beor*). Apparently horrified, he underlined the words, and in the margin, picking out the most distressing aspect of this deprivation, he wrote the single word "beor"!

If in turn this quotation is too frivolous, let me add another. In one of the manuscripts Parker owned we find a scribe heaving a sigh of relief at coming to the end of his stint. At the bottom of the text (CCCC 343, fol. 83^{v}) he writes:

> Explicit: expliciat.
> Scriptor ludere eat.
>
> (So it ends. Let it end.
> Let the Reader go off and enjoy himself.)

prouoked without any iust cause, to go to Rome to his holy
father. If any thyng went agaynst his mynde, then straygh-
way he woulde appeale to Rome to displease the prince: As
this lyghtnes of his, is uttered by a frende of his, wrytyng
unto hym, beyng at the seconde tyme (as he calleth it) in his
Edm.fo 187. exile, that he went away, sponte, nullo pænitus cogente,
neither feared with imprisonment, nor otherwyse tormen-
ted, nor that his sea was denyed unto hym: but only for one
VVilli. poore worde, spoken by one certaine man, named William,
warewaste. he determined to flee, and so by his fleeyng gaue the aduen-

a.

fiducia in tuos. Si ne urgeri anglia tam inopina
to hoste pigeret. quantum ingemisceres. quantum affe
ctares succurrere. uel subire nobiscum noua acer
bitatum genera. Sponte tua nullo penitus cogente
ereptus es periculis nostris. forsitan ne sentires que
nos perpeti. & quod grauius est spectare cogimur.
sullimari ad sacros ordines quosdam de curia
libus. quibus nec canonica electio. nec iusticia con
sensit. Quin dubium non est. si eosdem uerius ecclesie ostia

b.

Plate 48 *A defence of priestes mariages*: (a) In printed book SP 41, Parker inserted a cross-reference to (b), MS CCCC 452 p. 187, the text of Eadmer's *Historia novorum* (reduced)

fide spopondisse confessus est. Ait. Ego aplic' sum. & si feceris q'd po
stulo: ab hac te fidei sponsione absoluã. Tractabo de his ait. & que
consilii mei tenor inuenerit: paternitati tue notificabo. Hinc
a papa recessit. & ei p internuntios suos de negocio ita respon
dit. Quod dicit se qui aplic' est me a fide quã pollicit' sum abso
luturũ. si cont' eandẽ fidẽ Thurstanũ eboraci recepo: non ui
det' regie honestati conuenire. huiuscemodi absolutioni con
sentire. Quis enim fidẽ suã cuiuis polliceretur amplius crederet. cũ

a.

ter his councell holden at Remis, anno dñi. 1119. came vnto A
Gisortiũ, to speake with the king, & had conference with him.
Edmer. When the kyng had obteyned of that pope to haue all such
customes which his father had in England & in Normandie,
and especially of all other, that he should not suffer any man
to vse the office of a legate at any tyme in Englande, except
him selfe did require the same for such matters which coulde
not be ended by the byshop of Canterburie and the other
byshoppes of the Realme. All which thynges (sayth the sto-
rie) beyng thus determined, the pope doth make request to ye
kyng for his loue, to be frendly vnto Thurstone Archbyshop B
of Yorke, to restore hym to his Byshopricke. Whereunto
the kyng aunswered: that he woulde neuer do it whyle he
lyued, for (he saith) he hadde so promised vppon his fayth.
Wherupon Calixtus dyd aunswere. Ego apostolicus sum,
& si feceris quod postulo, ab hac te fidei sponsione absoluam.
I am in the apostles sea, and yf thou wylt do that which I
request, I wyl absolue thee from this promise of thy fidelitie.
Well sayth the kyng, I wyll entreate of this hereafter: and
shortly sent vnto hym his messengers, to signifie that it is
not for the kynges honour to consent to such absolutions a- C

b.

Plate 49 *A defence of priestes mariages*: (a) Parker used MS CCCC 452 p. 308 in the compilation of (b) printed book SP 41 p. 301 (reduced) worlde, and that he gaue hym three special gyftes, wisdome, ryches, and victorie, in such aboundaunce, that he excelled Edm.lib 6. (saith he) all his predecessours. Some proofe of his graces & good qualities may be considered, partly occasioned to be remembred by this foresayde archbishop Rodulph, who at a certaine coronation of the kynges newe wyfe Atheleida, daughter to Godefride duke of Lorayne, in the xxi. yere of his rayne, the sayde Rodulphus beyng the executor of the solempnitie at masse, and at the alter in his pontificalibus, castyng his eyes behynde hym, and seyng the sayde kyng syttyng on an hye throne with the crowne on his head, he went in a great haste from the alter vp to the kyng (whom he knewe was not crowned by hym or his predecessour) At whiche sodayne commyng, the kyng reuerentlye rose vp to hym: and the bysshop asked who had put on that crowne on

a.

b.

Plate 50 *A defence of priestes mariages*: (a) Parker's marginal notation in the printed text and (b) additional marginal cross-reference at corresponding point in MS CCCC 452

D cleane, and to lyue in secrete as they lust, and then all very well. With which banbery gloses, they hadde at the laste brought the open cleargie to renounce open auouchyng of their wyues, and lyued yet diuers of them secretelye with wyues of late dayes. For euen of late in archbishop Pec-chams dayes, they (after Othos decree of the same) styll pro-uided agaynst priestes chyldren, that they shoulde not nexte and

Pecham, anno.1281.

a.

b.

Plate 51 *A defence of priestes mariages*: (a) A marginal note in the printed text and (b) a corresponding marginal comment in MS CCCC 342 (reduced)

Plate 52 MS CCCC 191: John Joscelyn's annotation of part of the Old English text of the *Enlarged Rule of Chrodegang* (reduced)

In cunctis unum sunt tria principium.

¶ Cum pia mens in laude Dei superata labores,
Gaude, quod tantum te bene uincit opus.
Teq; aliquid superi cognosce hausisse uigoris,
Si tibi non satis est, quod cupis, atque sapis.
Quære bonum sine fine, bono & persiste reperto,
Quærere non habeant talia uota modum.
Nam qui se nullo iam munere credit egere,
Crescere non cupiens, perdit adepta tepens. D

Metrum anacreontium, quod & colopon dicitur, recipit anapæstum, duos iambos, & unam syllabam, ut, ăgĕ īām, prĕcōr, mĕā, rum.

Age iam precor mearum
Comes irremota rerum,
Trepidam, breuemq; uitam
Domino Deo dicemus.
Celeri uides rotatu
Rapidos dies meare,
Fragilisq; membra mundi
Minui, perire, labi.
Fugit omne, quod tenemus,
Neque fluxa habent recursum.
Cupidas, uagasq; mentes
Specie trahunt inani.
Vbi nunc imago rerum?
Vbi sunt opes potentum?

Quibus

Plate 53 Sixteenth-century annotations on p. 260 of CCCC B.4.16, verses by Prosper of Aquitaine. At least the bottom note in each margin is in Parker's hand (reduced)

Great riches wyde
And honors pride
  Adue I byd you be,
I wyll ensue
Good preuerke true
  Swete Christ suffiseth for me.

In wealth and wo
Betwixt them two
  I wyll so frame my mynde,
That neither wo
Shall greeue me so,
  Nor wealth shal make me blynd.

To Christ I wyll
With lyfe euen styll,
  Geue thankes and honor due,
Yet once agayne
I vowe it playne
  His prayse I wyll ensue.

pouert

Plate 54 MS CCCC 448: One of Parker's proof corrections to his translation of Prosper's verses

Plate 55 MS CCCC 198 fol. 218[r]: Part of the homily of *A testimonie of antiquitie* marked up in the margin to correspond to the printed text (reduced)

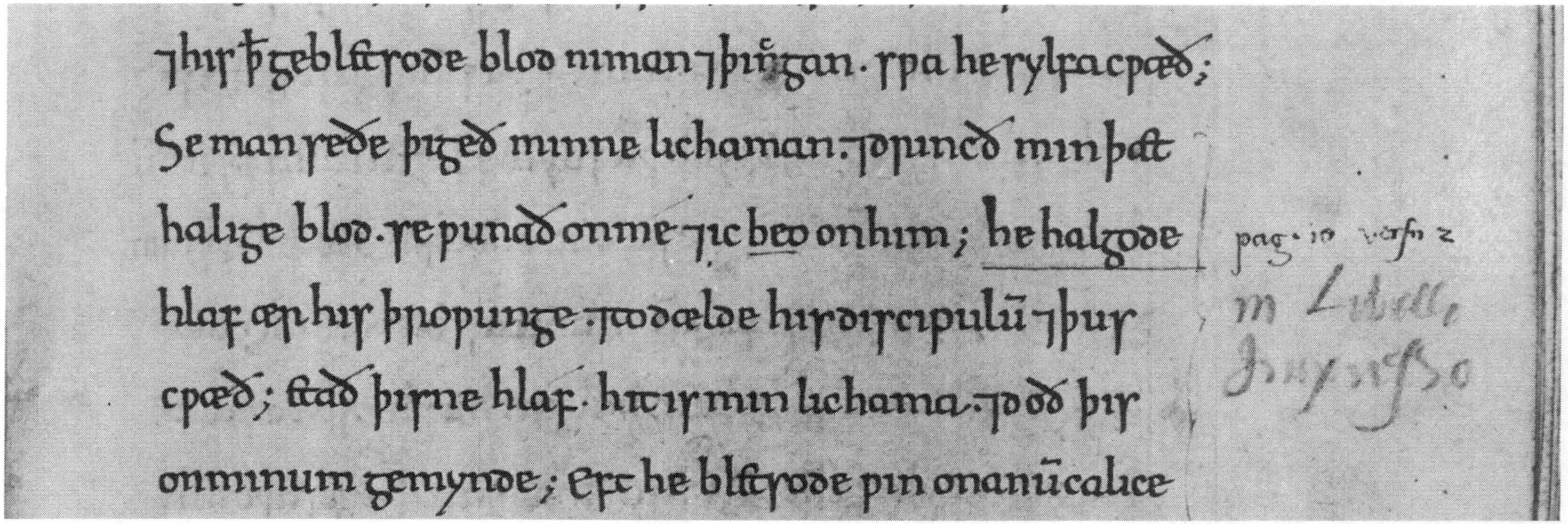

Plate 56 MS CCCC 162 p. 387: The Easter homily cross-referenced in the margin to the printed text of *A testimonie* . . .

þ his life is gelogod [dispositum / situm] on geswincum. Ðonne him hingrað.
he ett [comedit] gredeglice, ec þonne him þyrst. he drincð gif
he hæfð. þonne him celt he cepð him hleoþe [calorem]. Ðonne
him to gange lift he gæð on þannces hwyder þone he,
werig bið he wile hine restan. gif he gewundad bið,
he wilnað læcedomes. Nis his nu eall geswinc ⁊ gecte
micele, swarran ealle þaunge limpe he on þisum life
becunnað, þe man earfodlice mæg eall areccan [narrare] uton
forði hogian [studere] her on þisum life. þ we mid geornne [diligentia] ful-
nesse, ge wilnian æfre þæse beteran lifes on þære ecan
Blisse mid urum hælende criste swa swa he us behaten
hæfð. Se þe leofað ⁊ rixað mid his leofan fæder and
þam halganne gaste on anre god cundnysse ana [solus]
soðe scippende ealra þinga. Amen.

Finis examenon.

Plate 57 MS CCCC 178 p. 31: A supply leaf, probably in Matthew Parker's hand (reduced)

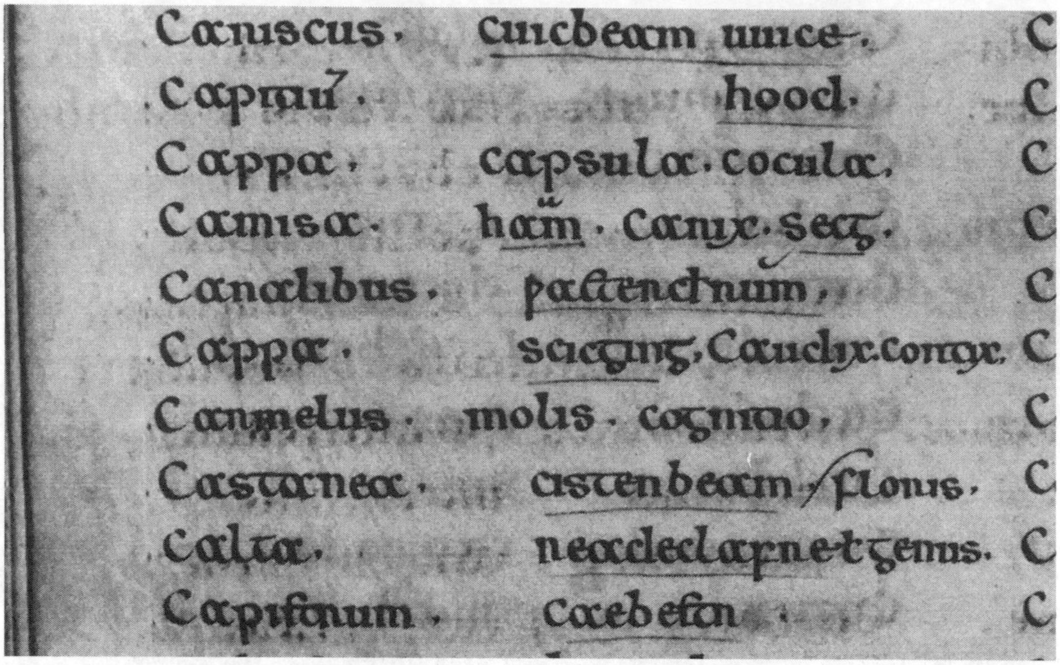

a.

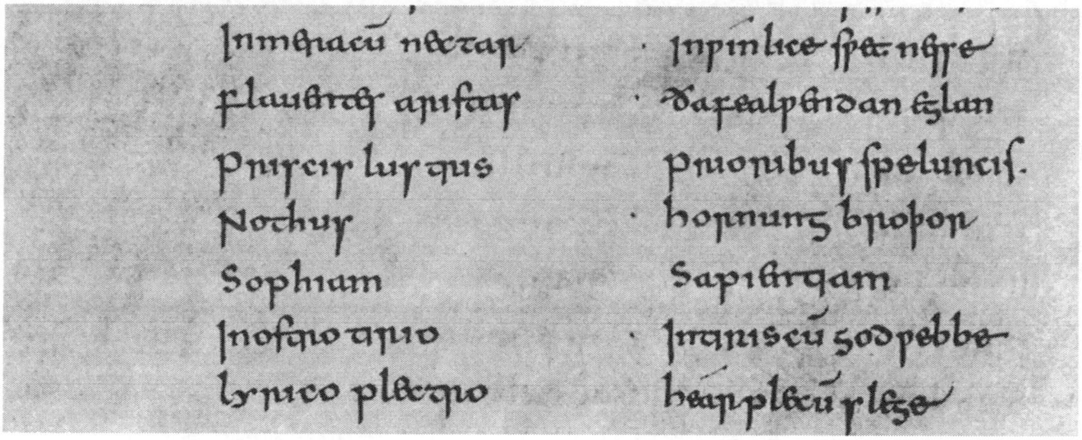

b.

Plate 58 Latin/Old English glossaries: (a) MS CCCC 144 fol. 14^{v}, extract from the *Corpus Glossary* with Old English glosses underlined for collection into a dictionary (actual size) and (b) MS CCCC 183 fol. 70^{v}, difficult Latin words with Latin or Old English equivalents (reduced)

Plate 59 MS CCCC 449 fol. 89r: A section of AElfric's *Glossary* marked up for collection of words into a dictionary

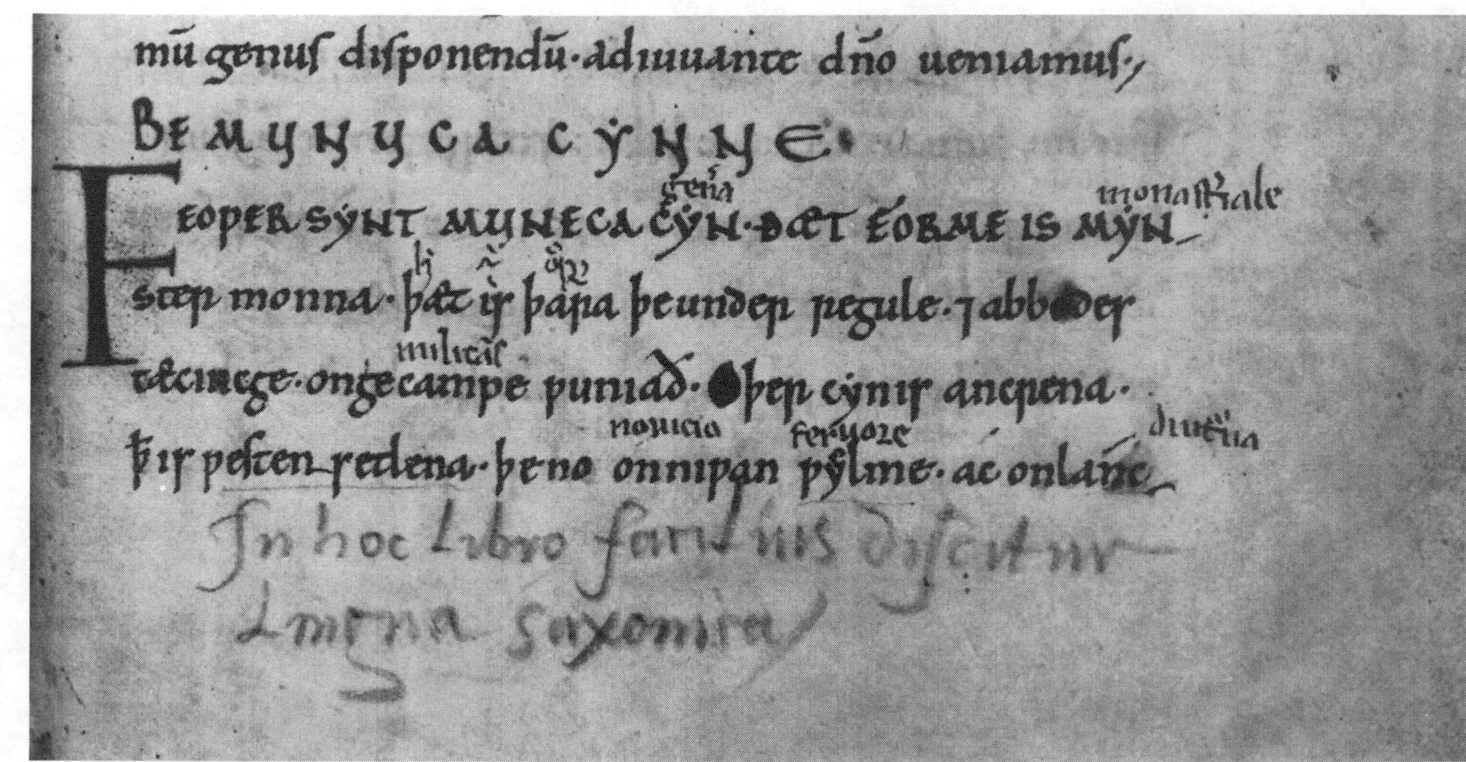

Plate 60 MS CCCC 178 p. 291: Parker used the bilingual Rule of St. Benedict to help himself learn Old English

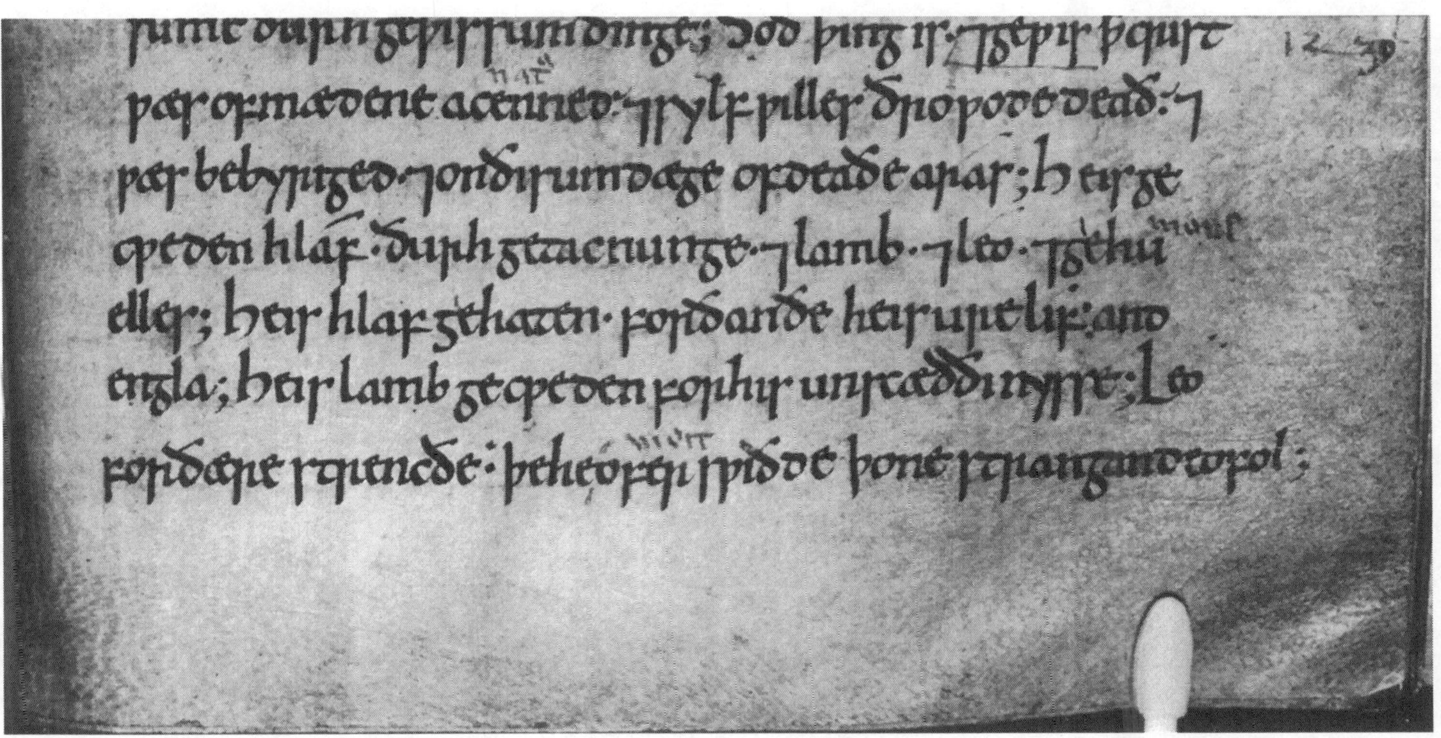

Plate 61 MS CCCC 198 fol. 220^{r}: The "tremulous Worcester Hand" errs in translating Old English

This is the Preface how S. Gregorie this booke made, which
Ðis is seo forespræc hu S. Gregorius þas boc gedihte þe
men the Pastoral doe call.
man Pastoralem nemnað.

Ælfred Kyng wysheth greetyng to Wulffige Bishop hys worthy
ÆLfred Kyning hateð gretung Wulfsige Biscop his wordum — alias gre-tun.
louely & frendly, & thee to know I wyll, that to me it cometh very often in
luflice ⁊ freondlice; ⁊ þe cyðan hate; ꝥ me com swiðe oft on
mynde what maner of wisemē lōg since were throughout the English nation, both of
gemynd; hwylce witan geo wæron geond Angelcyn; ægðer ge
the spirituall degree as of the temporaltie, & how happy the times thē were amōgst
godcundra hada ge woruldcundra; ⁊ hu gesæliglica tida þa wæron ge-
all the English nation, & how the kinges which than the gouernmēt had of the people,
ond Anglecyn; ⁊ hu þa cyningas þe þone anweald hæfdon þæs folces;
God & his will written they obeyed, & how they both in theyr peace
Gode ⁊ his ærendwritũ hyrsumodon; ⁊ hu hi ægðer ge heora sybbe
& in their expeditiō of war, & in their gouerning within borde or at home helde, &
ge heora sydo; ⁊ ge heora anweald innan borde gehealdon; ⁊
also without their noblenes did spread, & how they then sped, aswell in witte
eac ut hira eðel rymdon; ⁊ hu him þa speow; ægðer gemid wige
as in wisdome. And also the deuine orders how earnest they were aswell
gemid wisdome. And eac þa godcũdan hadas hu georne hi wæron ægðer
about preaching, and about learnyng, & about all the seruices that they
geymbe lara; geymbe leornunga; ⁊ ymbe ealle þa þeowdomas þe hi
to God should do. And how men out abroade wisdome & doctrine hither in this land
Gode sceoldon; ⁊ hu man ut on borde wisdome ⁊ lare hider on land
sought, & how we the same now must abroad get, if we them haue shall.
sohte; ⁊ hu we hi nu sceoldon ute begitan; gif we hi habbã sceoldõ.
So cleane it was fallen amongst the english nation, that very few were on
Swa clæne heo wæs oðfeallen on Angelcynne; ꝥ swiðe feawa wæron be
this side Humbre which their seruice could vnderstand in English,
heonan Humbre þe hira þenunge cuðon understandan on Englisc;
or els furthermore an epistle from latin into english to declare, & I
oððe furðon an ærendgewryt of ledene on Englisc areccan; ⁊ ic
wene that not many beyond Humbre were not. So few of them were,
wene ꝥ naht monige begeondã Humbre næron. Swa feawa heora wæron;
that I also one onely may not remember by south Thamise when as I
ꝥ ic furþon anne ænlepne ne mæg geþencan besuðan Thamise þa þa ic
to reigne vndertoke. God almighty be thanked, that we now any in stall
to rice feng. Gode ælmightigum sy þanc; ꝥ we nu ænigne an steal
haue a teacher. Therfore I thee bid that thou do as I beleue that thou wilt,
habbað lareowa. Forþam ic þe beode; ꝥ þu do swa ic gelyfe ꝥ þu wylle;
that thou with these worldly thinges to them powrest out, as thou oftnest mayest,
ꝥ þu þe þissa woruld þinga to þam geæmtige; swa þu oftost mæge;
that thou that wisdome which to thee God geueth wheresoeuer thou to them bestow
ꝥ þu þone wisdome þe þe God sealde þær þær þu hine befæstan
may thou bestow. Thinke what maner of punishmēts to vs then shall comen for this
mæge befæst; geþenc hwilce witu us þa becomon for þisse

F.j. woruld;

Plate 62 MS CCCC 176 F.j.: A section of the text and translation of Alfred's prefatory letter to his version of the *Cura pastoralis* as appended to some issues of Asser's *Life of Alfred* (reduced)

[illegible]

The Epistle of ~~King~~ Alfred to ~~[illegible]~~ Bishop

ALFRED Kynge lovely and frendly salutith the worthie bisshop ~~[illegible]~~
I will the to understande that very often it cometh into my remembraunce
how wise men were in tymes past throughout the whole englishe nation
as well of the clergie: as of the laytie: how happie tymes were then
throughout all England: how the kinges that had the rule of the
people did then obey god, and his messengers, and how they did well
mayntayne the peace, their kingdome, their castles (?) as well within as
without, and how they spedde both in warre, and in wisdome. Agayne
as touching clergy men also how diligent they were bothe to learne and
to teache, how peynfull about all dutie and service they shulde do unto
god, and how men beyonde the seas came hither to seke wisdome and
learnyng, and how we must now go seke it without if we will have
it. so utterly is it lost in our Englishe nation, that very fewe were
on this side humber that coulde understande their owne service in
Englishe, or also translate one Epistle from Latyn to Englishe, or
els (?) furthermore turne one writ out of Laten into englishe,
and I wene not many nether beyonde humber. so fewe truly there
were that I knowe not one only by southe Thames when I began
to reigne. God be thanked for that we have now in stall any teachers (?)
all. Wherfore I thinke the that thou do as I beleve thou wilt,
that thou which applyest thy selfe unto these worldlie thinges, so ofte
as thou maist, that the wisdome wch god hath geven the thou
bestowe where thou thinkest best. thinke what punyshment shal
come upon us for this worlde, when that we have neither loved
wisdome [illegible] nor have left and taught the same to other.

Plate 63 MS CCCC 197A p. 1: A page of an anonymous translation of Alfred's preface to the *Cura pastoralis* with heading in Parker's hand (reduced)

APPENDIX: MATTHEW PARKER'S HAND

N. R. Ker's assertion that Matthew Parker was too busy to annotate his manuscripts (see p. 87 above) is expanded by his comment on "notes and marks in the well-known and conspicuous red pencil used perhaps by Parker himself and certainly by his son John" (Ker 1957:liii). C. E. Wright had raised the matter some years earlier with a discussion of certain "red chalk markings and underlinings" which

> have usually been regarded as the work of the Archbishop himself, but the use of the same red chalk for pagination and rulings makes it unlikely that for this sort of tedious work the Archbishop would have time to spare. Some evidence seems to suggest a connexion with the Archbishop's son, John (Wright 1951:228).

John certainly used this pencil/chalk/crayon, but there can also be no doubt that Matthew annotated and underlined places in manuscripts in it. This can be seen clearly in archival manuscripts still in Corpus Christi College. Matthew Parker gave up the administration of the College in 1553 when John was only five, so it is unlikely that it was John who contributed to the Corpus archives. Whether by 1566 he would have been entrusted to annotate manuscripts needed for the publication of *A testimonie* . . . (see pp. 94–98 above) must remain uncertain. For that he would need, by the age of eighteen, some knowledge of both Latin and Old English.

Nevertheless the doubts that Ker and Wright express on the identification of Matthew Parker's hand in his manuscripts are salutary. We need to establish the characteristics of his hand, and for this must have a number and variety of accredited examples. The variety is necessary because, like many of us, Parker did not have a single script; it changed with age, purpose, and medium.

He had a cursive script that he used for day-to-day administrative affairs and for drafts of letters. This is often vouched for by his signature at the bottom of a document. He had a formal italic hand for formal purposes, for headings and titles of books, for entering his name on official documents. As yet we have not categorized this hand adequately. It is notoriously hard to identify individual italic hands with certainty, largely because their rigorous formal nature disguises personal characteristics. There is a similar problem in identifying Parker's secretary hand. But he also used a less formal hand, with both italic and cursive qualities, for annotating documents, for entries on flyleaves, and so on, and this is the one I have identified as Parker's in these lectures. These are often in ink, but a somewhat bolder version of the same hand occurs in the notes in red crayon or in pencil. Ker identifies this hand as Matthew Parker's in MS CCCC 173 (Ker:1957:lii), and M. R. James finds it in several manuscripts, such as CCCC 81 and 106. It was Parker who contributed the list of eminent men called Matthew in MS CCCC 101, p. 432, and it is reasonable to assume too that it was he who corrected the proof (if that is what it is) of *Prosper his meditation with his wife* and who improved the halting verse in his copy of his translation of the psalter (SP 1).

Such examples, accredited or virtually so, make it relatively easy to build up a corpus of Matthew Parker's manuscript annotations and so to identify his marginal *nota* marks by their association with such annotations. It is on the basis of material such as this that I have made my comments on Parker's use of his books. The characteristics of his semi-cursive script need further analysis, if only to help us isolate his italic hand. Dr. Mildred Budny has made a preliminary examination and lists among the significant graphs: the form of *f* as an initial; *s* shaped like an integral sign; *g* with a sweeping tail; *l* with an extended stem, an angular turn from it into the foot, and a short heel; *d* with a rounded bow and ascending curved back; *p* with a descending stem and a tail that loops back; and *e* sometimes in the Greek form.

BIBLIOGRAPHY

Adams 1967	Adams, H. M. *Catalogue of Books printed on the Continent of Europe, 1501–1600 in Cambridge libraries*. 2 vols. Cambridge: Cambridge University Press.
Bishop 1966	Bishop, T. A. M. "An early example of the square minuscule." *Transactions of the Cambridge Bibliographical Society*. 4/3:246–52.
Bromwich 1962	Bromwich, J. "The first book printed in Anglo-Saxon types." *Transactions of the Cambridge Bibliographical Society*. 3/4:265–91.
Bruce and Perowne 1853	Bruce, J. and T. T. Perowne. *Correspondence of Matthew Parker, D.D. Archbishop of Canterbury*. Cambridge: Parker Society.
Caius 1568	[Caius, J.]. *De antiquitate Cantabrigiensis academiæ libri duo*. London.

Cheney 1987	Cheney, C. R. "A register of MSS borrowed from a College library, 1440–1517: Corpus Christi College, Cambridge MS 232." *Transactions of the Cambridge Bibliographical Society*. 9/2:103–29.
Dumville 1987	Dumville, D. N. "Early square minuscule script: the background and earliest phases." *Anglo-Saxon England*. 16:147–79.
Foxe 1571	[Foxe, J.]. *The Gospels of the fower euangelistes translated in the olde Saxons tyme*. London.
Gaselee 1921	Gaselee, S. *The early printed books in the library of Corpus Christi College*, Cambridge: a hand-list. Cambridge: Cambridge University Press.
James 1899	James, M. R. *The sources of Archbishop Parker's collection of MSS at Corpus Christi College, Cambridge*. Cambridge: Cambridge Antiquarian Society Octavo Publications 32.
James 1912	James, M. R. *A descriptive catalogue of the manuscripts in the library of Corpus Christi College Cambridge*. 2 vols. Cambridge: Cambridge University Press.
James 1600	I[ames], T. *Ecloga Oxonio-Cantabrigiensis, tributa in libros duos*. London.
Ker 1957	Ker, N. R. *Catalogue of manuscripts containing Anglo-Saxon*. Oxford: Clarendon Press.
Ker 1964	Ker, N. R. *Medieval Libraries of Great Britain: a list of surviving books*. 2nd ed. London:

Royal Historical Society Guides and Handbooks 3.

Kotzor 1974 — Kotzor, G. "St. Patrick in the Old English 'Martyrology': on a lost leaf of MS. C.C.C.C. 196." *Notes and Queries*. NS 21:86–87.

Leinbaugh 1982 — Leinbaugh, T. H. "Ælfric's *Sermo de sacrificio in die pascae*: Anglican polemic in the sixteenth and seventeenth centuries." In *Anglo-Saxon scholarship: the first three centuries*, ed. C. T. Berkhout and M. M. Gatch, 51–68. Boston, Mass.: G. K. Hall and Co.

Madden 1866–69 — Madden, Sir Frederic. *Matthaei Parisiensis, monachi sancti Albani, historia Anglorum*. 3 vols. London: Rolls Series.

Masters 1753 — Masters, R. *The history of the College of Corpus Christi and the B.Virgin Mary (commonly called Bene't) in the University of Cambridge*. Cambridge.

Nasmith 1777 — Nasmith, J. *Catalogus librorum manuscriptorum quos Collegio Corporis Christi et B. Mariæ Virginis legavit . . . Matthæus Parker*. Cambridge.

Oates 1986 — Oates, J. C. T. *Cambridge University Library: a history: from the beginnings to the Copyright Act of Queen Anne*. Cambridge: Cambridge University Press.

Oldham 1952 — Oldham, J. B. *English blind-stamped bindings*. Sandars Lectures in Bibliography 1949. Cambridge: Cambridge University Press.

Page 1973 — Page, R. I. "Anglo-Saxon texts in early modern transcripts." *Transactions of the Cambridge Bibliographical Society*. 6/2:69–85.

Page 1983a — Page, R. I. "Matthew Parker's copy of *Prosper his meditation with his wife*." *Transactions of the Cambridge Bibliographical Society*. 8/3:342–49.

Page 1983b — Page, R. I. Review of Berkhout and Gatch (cf. Leinbaugh 1982). In *Notes and Queries*. NS 30:443–49.

Parkes 1976 — Parkes, M. B. "The palaeography of the Parker manuscript of the *Chronicle*, Laws and Sedulius, and historiography at Winchester in the late ninth and tenth centuries." *Anglo-Saxon England*. 5:149–71.

Plomer 1926–27 — Plomer, H. R. "The 1574 edition of Dr. John Caius's *De antiquitate Cantebrigiensis academiæ libri duo*." *Library*. 4 ser. 7:253–68.

Stanley 1722 — [Stanley, W.]. *Catalogus librorum manuscriptorum in bibliotheca Collegii Corporis Christi in Cantabrigia*. London.

Strongman 1977 — Strongman, S. "John Parker's manuscripts: an edition of the lists in Lambeth Palace MS 737." *Transactions of the Cambridge Bibliographical Society*. 7/1:1–27.

Strype 1711 — Strype, J. *The life and acts of Matthew Parker*. London.

Trahern 1973 — Trahern, J. B. "Amalarius *be becnum*: a fragment of the *Liber officialis* in Old English." *Anglia*. 91:475–78.

Vaughan 1958 — Vaughan, R. *Matthew Paris*. Cambridge: Cambridge Studies in Medieval Life and Thought NS 6.

Wanley 1705 — Wanley, H. *Antiquæ literaturæ septentrionalis liber alter*. Vol 2 of G. Hickes, *Linguarum vett. septentrionalium thesaurus*. Oxford.

Weale 1894–98 — Weale, W. H. J. *Bookbindings and rubbings of bindings in the National Art Library South Kensington Museum*. 2 vols. London.

Whitelock 1954 — Whitelock, D. *The Peterborough Chronicle (the Bodleian manuscript Laud Misc. 636)*. Early English Manuscripts in Facsimile 4. Copenhagen: Rosenkilde and Bagger.

Wright 1951 — Wright, C. E. "The dispersal of the monastic libraries and the beginnings of Anglo-Saxon studies," *Transactions of the Cambridge Bibliographical Society*. 1/3:208–37.

Wright 1967 — Wright, D. H. *The Vespasian Psalter (British Museum Cotton Vespasian A 1)*. Early English Manuscripts in Facsimile 14. Copenhagen: Rosenkilde and Bagger.